THE LEE BROS.

SIMPLE FRESH SOUTHERN

THE LEE BROS.

SIMPLE FRESH SOUTHERN

KNOCKOUT DISHES WITH DOWN-HOME FLAVOR

MATT LEE AND TED LEE

Photographs by Ben Fink

CLARKSON POTTER/PUBLISHERS

NEW YORK

Published in the United States by Clarkson Potter/Publishers, an imprint of
the Crown Publishing Group, a division of Random House, Inc., New York.
www.crownpublishing.com
www.clarksonpotter.com

CLARKSON POTTER is a trademark and POTTER with colophon is a
registered trademark of Random House, Inc.

Library of Congress Cataloging-in-Publication Data is available upon request.

ISBN 978-0-307-45359-4

Printed in China

Design by Stephanie Huntwork

10 9 8 7 6 5 4 3 2 1

First Edition

Simple Fresh Southern
is dedicated to
E.V. DAY
and to
GIA PAPINI LEE

contents

welcome

Welcome to *Simple Fresh Southern*—southern cooking that celebrates fresh ingredients used in creative ways, and that features quick-and-easy preparations with every bit as much southern soul as the long-simmered, the slow-smoked, and the deep-fried. Our style of cooking brooks no compromise on flavor or lusciousness: get ready for Pimento-Cheese Potato Gratin (page 155), Pork Tenderloins with Madeira and Fig Gravy (page 207), and Buttermilk Pudding Cakes with Sugared Raspberries (page 229).

We believe simple and fresh is the direction all southern home cooking is headed—for today's bounty of ingredients, for contemporary palates, and for the diverse modern diet. But we're inspired by southern traditions and ingredients, and often by our library of southern cookbooks. Many of these books were published in the mid-twentieth century and are beginning to show their age: the comb-bind on *Southern Sideboards* is brittle and cracking, a rubber band holds the pages of *Charleston Receipts* together, and *Natchez Recipes* (The Altar Guild of Trinity Episcopal Church, Natchez, MS, undated) is so delicate and frayed that we keep it in a plastic sleeve. Even so, these books are sources for many great simple, fresh, southern ideas. But the truth is, we rarely, if ever, cook directly from them.

So how does the inspiration come about?

Take, for example, Shrimp and Deviled-Egg Salad Rolls, on page 183. We were reading through *The New Fairyland Cooking Magic,* published by the Fairyland School PTA in Lookout Mountain, Georgia, in 1964 (Fairyland is pronounced FAIR-uh-lind, according to our dear friend Mary Calhoun, who grew up there), when we came across a recipe for "Shrimp–Deviled Egg Casserole." The recipe was, as you might imagine from the title, pretty far-out: it calls for making a batch of deviled eggs, and alternating layers of them in a casserole pan, topped up with a milky, roux-thickened cheese sauce studded with whole shrimp and spiked with ketchup, sherry, and Worcestershire sauce.

You cover all that with a carpet of butter-soaked bread crumbs, bake it for half an hour, and then serve it over "canned Chinese noodles that have been heated in a slow oven."

Wild, right?! But we've learned that whenever you find a puzzling recipe in an old southern cookbook, you can bet your cookie press there's a core of molten genius within. In this casserole, it's simply the marriage of shrimp and deviled eggs, a pairing made in some southern seaside idyll, and one that drove us into the kitchen to experiment.

What we developed was a simple egg salad with farm-fresh eggs, but one in which the binder had the depth of flavor and spice of our best deviled-egg filling. And then we folded in perfectly cooked, peeled local shrimp (chopped chunkily). We loved the shrimpy egg salad, which hit all the right comfort notes but wasn't over-the-top rich. A finishing flavor or two to round it out—a tonic squeeze of lemon (Ted's idea) and a crumble of smoky bacon and scallion (Matt's)—was all that was required. And the more we tasted the dish, the more it seemed to be the Lowcountry cousin to the lobster salad that gets tucked into toasted hot-dog buns and served as "lobster rolls" in roadside joints along the New England coast in summer. And there we had it: Shrimp and Deviled-Egg Salad Rolls, a recipe that's become a favorite of ours for casual summer suppers at the beach, or for an exquisite Sunday brunch sandwich any time of the year.

What we made of that casserole recipe is a dish we'd like to think has a claim to originality: odds are you haven't cooked one of these before! It's also a lighter dish that takes about a third as long to cook as the original, using half as many ingredients. And yet ours is a recipe with more flavor—not only brighter flavors, but layers of flavor. We think it's "restaurant-quality," but we're just home cooks. We've never worked in a restaurant kitchen; we make few assumptions about tools and equipment, or things like "knife skills," so our recipes are easy for every home cook. We're living proof that if you love cooking at home and are open-minded enough (and restless enough!) not to follow recipes to the letter, you can make soul-stirring food today.

Not every recipe in *Simple Fresh Southern* came from an idea we mined from our cookbook library. Sometimes, as in our Sweet Potato and Okra Fritters with Garlic Buttermilk Dip, page 86, they arose from a meditation, over time, on a beautiful southern pairing. Others, like Mint Julep Panna Cotta, page 245, hit like a bolt of lightning. But inevitably, each recipe in this book comes from a *Simple Fresh Southern* perspective, so in welcoming you to our kitchen, we thought we'd show you a little bit more about the three principles that guide the way we cook.

SIMPLE In our last book, *The Lee Bros. Southern Cookbook,* the shorthand "QKO," for "Quick Knockout," signaled a recipe that took no more than 30 minutes to make. We found in the eighteen months that we toured the United States—teaching cooking classes, lecturing, and demonstrating recipes from the book—that the QKOs were the recipes readers made most frequently. It makes sense: as much as we cherish the days we get to take our sweet time in the kitchen, they tend to come along much less frequently than the times we're really hustling to get things done and served on schedule so that the rest of life can rumble forward.

This book is guided by kitchen simplicity rather than by a strict adherence to preparation times or numbers of ingredients. It would be wonderful if every recipe cooked in the twenty minutes it takes to make our Crispy-Skin Salmon with Buttermilk-Mint Sauce, page 178, a perfect after-work entrée that uses only five ingredients (okay, six if you include salt). But we've also included recipes that may take a bit longer—a resting period, a cooling-down time, or a marination—yet require very little of the home cook and yield huge rewards with a minimum of kitchen prep and cleanup. For example, our Whole Roasted Chicken, page 193, which rests directly on a bed of carrots, onions, and potatoes in a skillet (no roasting rack required!), takes a little more than an hour to cook, but that time is fuss-free. And since you end up with not only a perfectly cooked chicken but also a roasty-warm side dish—all with minimal cleanup—the recipe qualifies in our book as a simple one. We evaluated the simplicity of each recipe based on how easily—from shopping to preparation, cooking to cleanup—it would integrate into the busy lives of home cooks.

FRESH "Fresh" has two senses in our cookbook. In the most literal, it means that we cook with the freshest ingredients we can find in our hometown, Charleston, South Carolina, and that we include shopping notes in our recipes to guide you to locating great ingredients and caring for them. Although you'll discover that we judiciously use store-bought mayonnaise, canned broth, frozen peas, and Tabasco sauce, we don't use processed foods such as condensed soups or dressing mixes. Freshness guides the choices and decisions we make about where and when to shop. Whenever possible, we hit the Tuesday farmers market in Mt. Pleasant and the Saturday market downtown on Marion Square. And we'll go a little bit out of our way, for example, to the Piggly-Wiggly on Meeting Street, which stocks a brand of shucked oysters from Bluffton, South Carolina. True, the Harris-Teeter on East Bay Street is a few blocks closer, but its shucked oysters come from farther away (Virginia).

So we use local produce, fish, and meats as much as we can, and we're attentive to seasonality. It makes us feel good when we can pull it off, but we don't obsess too much about it if we can't. In a perfect world, we'd eat only vegetables grown on our farm, seafood harvested from the end of our dock, and meats from animals raised on grasses grown in the pastures beyond our kitchen window. But in the real world (where we have neither farm, nor dock, nor pastures), it's just not possible. As food writers and as cookbook authors, we spend a lot of time touring the country, shopping for ingredients to use in our cooking classes, so we're aware that farmers markets and supermarkets vary in accessibility and quality from place to place. But we firmly believe that all *Simple Fresh Southern* recipes can be accomplished beautifully in towns from coast to coast.

There's a second meaning of "fresh" in our book, and it refers to a freshness in outlook: a new and original use of a timeless ingredient, as in our Buttermilk Fresh Cheese, page 93, and our Squid with Watermelon and Basil, page 89. Sometimes that freshness manifests itself as a new direction for a familiar southern standard, such as Red Rice Salad, page 141, and Rice Pudding Pops, page 237. And other times, we're just looking for a quick-and-easy treatment of a southern classic, as in our Easy Shrimp Creole, page 204, or our Easy Chicken and Dumplings, page 181.

If you've eaten in some of the better—not fancier, but *better*—restaurants around the South, perhaps you've discovered dishes with a similar spirit: Andrea Reusing's pork belly with pumpkin preserves at Lantern in Chapel Hill; or Scott Peacock's butterbean hummus at Watershed in Decatur; or Hugh Acheson's river trout with boiled-peanut sauce at Five and Ten in Athens; or Robert Stehling's creamed collards at Hominy Grill in Charleston. We get a tremendous amount of inspiration from these chefs, and we bet that their recipes might be adaptable to home cooking. But we assure you, no background in restaurant dining, or even in southern food, really, is assumed in this book, and no expertise is required to make your *Simple Fresh Southern* meals a success.

SOUTHERN What *is* southern?

After all, the way people cook in Charleston differs from the way people cook in Asheville, and in Richmond, and in Chattanooga, and in Dothan, and in Tallahassee. To complicate matters further, many of the ingredients and dishes we think of when we think "southern"—from collard greens to fried chicken to pecan pie—these days are grown and prepared throughout North America.

We know this: southern ingredients are our starting point, our palette, so to speak. And we're guided by the spectrum of southern flavors, from the playful sweet-sour brightness of relishes and pickles to the greener taste of freshly shelled peas, butterbeans, mint, and parsley, to savory meats, from the smoky funk of good barbecued pork to the salty-sweetness of blue crabs picked straight from the shell. And we know southern techniques from reading great classic southern cookbooks, from Mary Randolph to Mrs. S. R. Dull, our cherished community books, put out by altar guilds and Junior Leagues, and those by luminaries like Edna Lewis, Bill Neal, and Jean Anderson.

Our reliance upon fresh ingredients and simplicity in *Simple Fresh Southern* may resemble the old ways more than anything—a time before the rise of mid-century convenience foods. But it doesn't end there. We've always thought the hallmark of twentieth-century southern cooking is its spirited resourceful-ness—turning thrift into indulgence with a wink. Saving leftover watermelon-rind pickle brine to make a salad dressing or a ham glaze? *Very* southern. But what if that pickle brine came not from a traditional rind pickle (with its four-day soak in pickling lime) but from our Watermelon and Onion Pickles, page 71, that we make in ten minutes with Scrabble-tile-size squares of red seedless watermelon and crushed red chile? *Southern?* What if we smoke cauliflower in a stovetop smoker and puree it with buttermilk on page 166 to make a killer side dish. *Southern?* We char green beans in a skillet on page 148 and douse them with a sweet-tart dressing of fresh orange, vinegar, and orange zest. *Southern?* We use fresh South Carolina–grown soybeans in our Cherry Tomato and Soybean Salad, page 121. *Is that southern?*

Our answer to all these questions is, "Hell, *yes!*" But truly, an individual litmus test of southernness wouldn't matter. Southern soul doesn't come from any one thing, whether it's a mayonnaise jar, a deep-fryer, or even a quail trap; it's a far more complex and wondrous cocktail of traditions, techniques, ingredients, and flavors. Still, we enjoy asking that question of our cooking, because in doing so, we seem to open the door to new possibilities. It's how we move the discussion forward, and make better southern food. In the *Simple Fresh Southern* kitchen, we firmly believe southern cooking is a living art, one that is ever on the increase, with the potential to cast a spell on the wide world.

cocktails and coolers

In our first cookbook we made the claim that southerners brought a special mojo to crafting their desserts, but we should issue a correction: southerners have a gift for composing both fun desserts *and* drinks. And the beverages don't have to be sweet like dessert—or alcoholic, for that matter—to be interesting. Outside the standard iced tea, beer, and wine there is plenty of territory to conquer, so here we present a small sampling of the drink ideas we're loving now, from a ginger-spiced lemonade to a souped-up rum and coke to a chocolate milkshake that is decidedly not for kids.

Fasten your seat belts. For many of you this is going to be the first time you've seen the words *Purple* and *Jesus* next to each other, and you wine enthusiasts may never have contemplated letting a wine cooler pass your lips, but if you give us a few minutes of your time, we promise that our recipes—even the silliest sounding ones—deliver finely articulated flavors, well-calibrated textures, and an extra jolt of vivacity that comes from using fresh fruits and vegetables (yes, see the Celery Julep, page 36). Our plentiful variations multiply the possibilities and occasionally offer a few ways to detoxify or fortify these drinks.

Southerners who pride themselves on good hospitality know that nothing jazzes up an everyday occasion, or burnishes a reputation, like an original and delicious beverage.

WINE COOLERS: TANGERINE, STRAWBERRY, AND HONEYDEW (PAGE 27)

RECIPES

Strawberry Wine Coolers

Applejack Punch

Watermelon Margaritas

Ginger Lemonade

Hummers

Celery Julep

Peach Iced Tea

Lowcountry Pousse-Rapière

Spiced Rum-n-Cokes

Purple Jesus ("PJ")

STRAWBERRY WINE COOLERS

serves 6 • TIME: 15 minutes

Wine coolers are potentially one of the best ideas going—the combination of wine and fruit is pure genius—and yet the reality of a commercial wine cooler is pathetic. You must remember those: they're a candy-colored, sweetened gateway booze for seventh-graders. Whatever's in them, it sure ain't wine. Eager to reclaim wine coolers for adult consumption, we concocted this strawberry formula made with fresh berries buzzed in a blender, and encouraged by our success, went on to create the honeydew and tangerine variations that follow. Like a good sangria, these recipes marry the flavors of the wine and the fruit in a way that's balanced, luscious, and off-dry, but still interesting, with the flavor of real fruit and a nice kick. They're super-colorful too. For larger parties and barbecues, we prepare all three variations, whose pink-green-orange colors look coloring-book cute. Enjoy, but definitely keep an eye on the kids.

1 pound fresh strawberries (not frozen), rinsed and hulled 2 ounces vodka	Generous pinch of kosher salt (essential, not optional)	Two 750 ml bottles off-dry white wine, such as an American-grown Riesling, chilled

1 Keep 6 strawberries for garnish. Combine the rest of the strawberries, the vodka, the salt, and 1¾ cups of the wine in a blender, and puree on the highest setting for about 1 minute, until smooth and frothy. Strain the mixture through a coarse-mesh strainer or colander into a quart-size pitcher to remove any large bits of pulp. Agitate and press the mash in the strainer with a wooden spoon to release as much liquid as possible. (Chef gets first dibs on the strawberry pulp foam, which is best eaten directly from the strainer.) Serve immediately, or if time permits, cover the pitcher with plastic wrap and refrigerate for 2 hours.

2 To serve, fill 6 large wineglasses with ice cubes and pour in the strawberry mixture until each glass is only half full. Top each glass with a couple splashes of cold wine, stir with a clean index finger, and garnish with a split strawberry on the rim of the glass.

honeydew wine coolers Substitute 1 pound cubed honeydew melon (about 3 cups) for the strawberries.

tangerine wine coolers In this blender-less variation, we use 2 cups of hand- or machine-squeezed fresh tangerine juice blended with ½ cup water in place of the strawberries. Mix this directly in the pitcher with the vodka, the salt, and the 1¾ cups wine, and skip the straining step. If you have access to a blender and don't mind cleaning it, then pulse the mixture for a minute to aerate the brew and thicken the cooler before pouring it into the ice-filled glasses, and topping them off with the cold white wine.

red strawberry wine coolers Instead of topping up the glasses with the white wine in the final step, top them with a couple splashes of a chilled dry red wine to intensify the color, reduce the sweetness, and bring out a more complex, sangria-like flavor.

APPLEJACK PUNCH

Our apple cocktail marries two of the Western Hemisphere's finest spirits, applejack and rum, in a drink that is fundamentally dry and elegant but has a nice sweet-and-sour kick. The apple impression comes through in a subtle way—a shot of pure juice reinforced by the faint apple flavor of the applejack, which is simply a brandy distilled from apples, akin to Normandy's calvados or Brittany's lambig.

Applejack is America's oldest native-grown spirit, much more significant to the cultural life of the early republic than we might imagine, considering its barely perceptible standing today in a crowded field of vodkas, gins, and whiskeys.

None other than George Washington himself was responsible for turning the state of Virginia on to applejack in the latter half of the eighteenth century, and in the 1830s Abraham Lincoln served applejack—among other beverages—in his Springfield, Illinois, tavern. Today Laird and Company, of Scobeyville, New Jersey, is the sole American firm producing apple brandy, and most retailers and many bars stock a bottle of Laird's Applejack (though you may have trouble convincing the proprietor to locate it). Using a French apple brandy in this recipe is unpatriotic but will result in a more pronounced apple flavor, since these days Laird and Company dilutes their applejack somewhat with neutral spirits.

This cocktail is composed of equal parts crushed ice and punch, so that the ice partially melts into the concentrated brew, creating a slushy drink. Freeze it further after blending and pack in a thermos for transporting to a picnic, or double the recipe for a party and serve it in a punch bowl, floating a whole green apple in it to telegraph the main ingredient.

---

1 cup apple cider	8 ounces (1 cup) dark rum, such as Mount Gay or Myers's, chilled	4 dashes Angostura bitters (optional)
½ teaspoon grated lemon zest		Seltzer water or club soda
2 tablespoons fresh lemon juice	10 ounces (1¼ cups) Laird's Applejack or a calvados or lambig, chilled	
3 tablespoons dark or light brown sugar		

In a pitcher, mix the cider, lemon zest and juice, brown sugar, rum, and applejack together. Stir vigorously for several seconds to dissolve the sugar. Fill each of four 8-ounce rocks glasses to the top with crushed ice, and divide the punch evenly among the glasses, garnishing each with a dash of bitters and a splash of seltzer.

WATERMELON MARGARITAS

serves 8 • TIME: 15 minutes

The perfect drink for steamy summer evenings on the porch. We tame the deliciously syrupy sweetness of watermelon juice with lime juice and tequila to make a margarita so balanced and easy-drinking, you'll need to watch yourself (and the porch railing!). Note that if you let it sit, the watermelon juice separates into a thick red pulp and a clearer liquid; since you want the pulp to give this drink luxurious body, be sure to whisk up the juice thoroughly before pouring it into the shaker.

4 pounds seedless watermelon	16 ounces (2 cups) fresh lime juice (from about 16 small limes)	8 ounces (1 cup) Triple Sec, Cointreau, or other orange liqueur
Eight 1-inch-long strips lime peel		
Kosher salt	16 ounces (2 cups) tequila blanco ("silver tequila")	

1 Cut the flesh from the melon (discard the rind), chop it into chunks, and transfer it, in batches if necessary, to a food processor or blender. Liquefy the watermelon. You should have about 1 quart watermelon juice.

2 For each cocktail, salt the rim of an 8-ounce glass by first smearing it with a piece of lime peel and then dipping it in a saucer of kosher salt. Fill a cocktail shaker with ice, and add 4 ounces (½ cup) of the watermelon juice, 2 ounces (¼ cup) lime juice, 2 ounces tequila, and 1 ounce orange liqueur. Shake vigorously and strain into the glass. Garnish with the lime peel.

cool it down!

watermelon lime cooler If you're the abstemious type, omit the alcohol in this drink, pour it over ice, and you've got a really delicious summer cooler. You may want to add a splash of seltzer to make it a little less sticky. You'll see what we mean.

GINGER LEMONADE

serves 8 • TIME: 10 minutes steeping, 5 minutes preparation

I f we were musicians, we'd write a torch song about ginger and lemon, a match made in heaven. And though we've been drinking fresh lemonade as long as we can remember (Coca-Cola was taboo at 83 East Bay Street), we never thought to make a cold fresh-ginger lemonade until recently. Now we're making up for lost time. This drink is easy to make, super-refreshing, and happens to be a kick-ass mixer with bourbon and tequila, so those of you who are of age should mix up the Ginger Lemon Drop and the Lemon Gingerita variations that follow.

2 ounces fresh ginger, peeled, cut into thin disks (⅓ cup)	¼ cup honey, or more to taste ⅛ teaspoon kosher salt	¾ cup fresh lemon juice (from about 4 large lemons)

1 Put the ginger in a medium heatproof bowl. Bring 2 cups cold water to a boil, then pour it into the bowl and stir to agitate the ginger. Slowly pour in the honey, stirring until it's dissolved in the concentrate. Add the salt, cover, and let steep for 10 minutes.

2 Strain the concentrate into a large pitcher (it will keep for 5 days, covered, in the refrigerator), reserving the ginger slices. Add 3 cups cold water and the lemon juice to the pitcher, and sweeten to taste with honey. Set the pitcher in the refrigerator to cool further; store the ginger slices in the refrigerator as well. (The lemonade and ginger slices will keep in the refrigerator for 5 days.)

3 Fill each highball or pint glass two-thirds of the way to the rim with ice, and pour the ginger lemonade over it. Garnish with a slice of the steeped ginger.

NOTE If, after making Ginger Lemonade, you'd like to sweeten the lemonade further without adding more honey flavor, add superfine sugar to taste.

CELERY JULEP

serves 6 • TIME: 15 minutes

Whenever you've got a mess of celery tops or a few fading celery ribs that you're about to toss in the compost, make celery syrup with them instead. It's an inexpensive way to add intriguing herbal flavor to all kinds of desserts and drinks, from fruit salad to this garden-tweaked bourbon cocktail.

"Sweet celery?" you're probably thinking. Well, yes, and it's not just us. Dr. Brown's Cel-Ray soda, a fizzy, celery-flavored beverage, has been made since 1869 in Greenpoint, Brooklyn. It's a superb mixer, too, and by far the best Cel-Ray cocktail we've tasted is the "Harrison Tonic" at The Harrison restaurant in New York City. Composed of Cel-Ray, bourbon, and lemon juice, it flatters the southern spirit in a manner so much more compelling than cola, more beguiling even than mint.

We've never found a reliable source for Cel-Ray in Charleston—and in fact the soda seems to be on the wane even in Brooklyn—but no matter: you can make celery syrup in a flash and stir up this julep wherever you happen to live.

10 ounces celery (about 4 large ribs)	12 ounces (1½ cups) Kentucky bourbon or Tennessee whiskey	12 ounces (1½ cups) seltzer water or club soda (optional)
½ cup plus 1 tablespoon sugar	¼ cup plus 2 tablespoons fresh lemon juice (from 2 to 3 lemons)	Celery tops, for garnish (optional)
½ teaspoon celery seeds		
¼ teaspoon kosher salt		

1 Chop the celery into pieces, put them in a food processor with 1 tablespoon of the sugar, the celery seeds, and the salt, and process until the celery is a loose purée. Pass the liquid through a fine-mesh strainer, pressing the pulp to extract as much flavor as possible. You should have about ⅓ cup.

2 Add the celery juice and remaining sugar to a small saucepan, and warm the mixture over medium heat just until the sugar dissolves. You should have about 1 cup celery syrup. (Covered with plastic wrap, the syrup will keep in the refrigerator for 1 week.)

3 Fill six 9-ounce julep cups to the rim with crushed ice. Add 2 ounces bourbon, a tablespoon of lemon juice, and 2 to 2½ tablespoons of celery syrup to each glass, and stir. Top up with seltzer, if desired, and garnish with the celery tops if using.

PEACH ICED TEA

serves 8 • TIME: 20 minutes preparation, 45 minutes refrigeration

We drink gallons of iced tea year-round, and like most southerners, we drink it sweet. But in the summer months we add sunny-syrupy flavor by stirring in peaches that we've liquefied in a blender. The tree-ripened peaches we get from Sanders Peach Stand in Filbert, South Carolina, have such an intense, honeyed sweetness that this tea needs no added sugar whatsoever. If you use unripe peaches or ones that have been trucked in from far away, you may need to add a teaspoon or so of sugar or honey, as you wish.

6 regular-size bags Lipton, Luzianne, or other orange pekoe black tea	1 pound ripe freestone peaches, pitted (skins left on) and cut into wedges

1 Bring 2 cups cold water to a boil in a saucepan or kettle. Put the tea bags in a heatproof pitcher and pour the boiling water over them. Let steep for 15 minutes.

2 While the tea steeps, put the peaches in a food processor and process for about a minute and a half, until they have become a smooth, thick liquid.

3 Press the tea bags gently against the side of the pitcher with a wooden spoon to extract the liquid remaining in the bags, and discard the bags. Add 4 cups cold water. Stir in the peach puree, and refrigerate for 45 minutes.

4 Strain the tea through a fine-mesh strainer or a folded-over piece of cheesecloth into a serving pitcher. Keep refrigerated until ready to serve (or for up to 3 days).

5 Pour the tea into tall glasses filled two-thirds to the rim with ice cubes.

get your drink on!

peach tea julep For each cocktail, pour 4 ounces (½ cup) Peach Iced Tea into a rocks glass filled with ice cubes. Add an ounce of your favorite bourbon or Jack Daniel's Tennessee Whiskey. Garnish with a slice of fresh peach.

LOWCOUNTRY POUSSE-RAPIÈRE

serves 4 • TIME: 5 minutes

A *pousse-rapière*—"rapier's thrust" in French—is a champagne cocktail, invented in Gascony, that consists of dry champagne kissed with a small amount of Armagnac, a brandy distilled in the region. Though the name implies a thin, sharp, deadly drink, this fizzy cocktail is anything but: imagine an invigorating sip of racy, dry champagne followed by a mellow sweet-fruit note. It's rounded, baroque, life-affirming.

Our Lowcountry take on the cocktail substitutes a dose of plum brandy syrup from the jar of the brandied plums we keep in the fridge (we garnish the drink with a slice or two of brandied plum). We pour it whenever life seems crushingly humdrum—a pile of dirty laundry to wash, or an afternoon of long-overdue vacuuming ahead—but it's also a knockout aperitif on special occasions, and nicely lower in alcohol than a spirit-laden cocktail. Your guests can still hold up their end of the conversation come dinnertime.

Don't break the bank on fine champagne for the Lowcountry pousse-rapière—after all, you'll be doctoring the champagne with plum brandy. What's required is a lively sparkling wine, and there are plenty of inexpensive ones in the marketplace—for delicious deals, look for cavas from Spain, proseccos from Italy, or mousseux from France's Loire Valley. We've found the excellent Italian prosecco Zardetto on sale for $3.99 a bottle!

¼ cup Brandied Plum syrup (see page 232)	I whole Brandied Plum (page 232), cut into slender wedges, for garnish	One 750 ml bottle dry sparkling white wine

Pour the plum syrup into 4 champagne flutes or wineglasses, and add a wedge or two of brandied plum to each. Top up with the sparkling wine, and serve.

SPICED RUM-N-COKES

A little spice and citrus (and a really rumsy, caramel-tinted rum, like Mount Gay) make all the difference in our amped-up version of rum and coke— or Cuba Libre, if you prefer. Many colas seem to hint at clove flavor already, so we make it explicit by marinating 25 of the dried flower buds known as cloves (*Syzigium aromaticum,* native to Indonesia), and some strips of orange peel in the rum. After a couple hours, the alcohol dissolves the clove and orange oils, liberating them for deployment in this awesome tropical cocktail. The effect is subtle, elegant, and worth the tiny bit of effort.

I navel orange	One 750 ml bottle wood-aged 80- to 90-proof rum, such as Mount Gay or Barbancourt 8-year	Two 12-ounce cans cola
25 whole cloves, selected for the longest stems		2 limes, cut into wedges, for garnish (optional)

1 Slice the orange crosswise into ¾-inch-thick disks. Then, using a paring knife, remove the peel in a single strip from the three largest disks. Stud each peel down its center line with cloves, every ¾ inch or so, until it resembles a punk wristband. Eat the orange, and then trim a few curls of spare orange peel to use as garnish.

2 Place the clove-studded peels in the bottom of a carafe or pitcher, and decant the rum into the carafe, reserving the bottle and its cap for later. Allow the rum to marinate for 2 hours.

3 Decant the contents of the carafe back into the bottle. Discard the orange peels.

4 To serve, fill tall slender glasses or faceted cocktail tumblers with ice cubes, and add 2 or 3 ounces of the seasoned rum to each glass. Top with cola, and garnish with a curl of orange peel and a lime wedge. (The leftover seasoned rum will keep for a year or more.)

PURPLE JESUS ("PJ")

serves 8 • TIME: 10 minutes preparation, overnight marination

Ah, where to begin? In the South, and especially on college campuses, a popular party trick is to fill a bathtub or plastic garbage can with "Purple Jesus," a blend of rotgut liquor, citrus fruit, and grape Kool-Aid. It's a colorful tradition, which begins festively enough and rarely ends well. There are many variations on the formula—adding a high-top sneaker to the brew is customary in certain subregions.

Our version embraces the basic flavor profile of Purple Jesus but brings it out of the frat house and into the faculty club. We like to compare the flavor of our vodka-based PJ to a homemade Campari, with deep and bold black-fruit flavors, an appetizingly bitter edge, and an affinity for blending with sparkling water.

8 ounces cherries, preferably black	½ grapefruit	One 750 ml bottle vodka
1 navel orange	1 pint blackberries, rinsed and shaken dry	Seltzer water or club soda, for serving

1 Keep 8 cherries, stems on, aside for garnish. Stem, halve, and pit the rest. Put the pitted cherry halves in a large carafe or pitcher. Cut 8 thin curls of orange peel from the orange, and set them aside in a small covered dish in the refrigerator. Peel the orange and the grapefruit; slice the fruits crosswise, and add to the pitcher along with the blackberries. Pour in the vodka. Cover, and refrigerate overnight.

2 Strain the vodka and discard the fruit. Fill cocktail glasses with ice, and pour 2 to 3 ounces of the vodka into each glass. Top with a couple splashes of seltzer, and garnish with a curl of orange peel and a whole cherry. (PJ will keep for 2 weeks in the fridge.)

VARIATIONS

pj martini Pour 6 ounces of strained PJ into a cocktail shaker half full of cracked ice, and shake it for 15 seconds. Strain into 2 martini glasses.

pj smooth Stem and pit all the cherries, peel and segment the orange and grapefruit, and after steeping the mixture overnight, puree all the ingredients in a blender. This will increase the yield (and the fiber content). Serve on the rocks in tall glasses.

budget campari In developing our PJ recipe, we found that a near approximation of the flavor of the popular Italian *aperitivo* could be obtained with these same ingredients by making just a few changes to amplify the bitterness: do not peel the citrus before slicing, and use 1 whole grapefruit, instead of a half. Steep the ingredients for a full 24 hours in the fridge before straining. Unlike Campari, this brew must be kept refrigerated.

snacks and appetizers

Set a platter of smoked peel-and-eat shrimp down in front of a screen—whether it's Super Bowl Sunday and you've gathered neighbors from a ten-house radius, or you're viewing a movie on your laptop with your loved one—and watch attention wander toward the food.

This chapter is all about luscious, showstopping grazing foods: Garlic-Chile Crabs (page 49), Sweet Potato and Okra Fritters (page 86), Salt-and-Pepper Shrimp (page 84). We also include impressive dishes to roll out on any occasion, like Clams with Sweet Potato, Smoked Sausage, and Watercress (page 56), or Squid with Watermelon and Basil (page 89), or Skillet-Roasted Quail with Wilted Spinach (page 53). These are dishes you could just as easily turn into a weeknight main course, too, simply by dialing up the quantity.

You'll also find in this chapter a gathering of easy pickle recipes. We always keep an assortment in the fridge, for impromptu cocktail-hour pickle-and-ham plates, and because they so easily become the spark that ignites all kinds of meals, from the tartar sauce, made with chopped pickles, that spins your mind fish-wise to the Fried Green Tomato and Onion Pickles (page 77) that are great as a snack, on sandwiches, or scattered on salads.

The South has always been a great grazing culture—this is well established; witness our way with pimento cheese, boiled peanuts, and fried pork rinds. We think the recipes in this chapter fit into that tradition of easy-to-love edibles with the potential to expand the empire of southern food worldwide.

CLOCKWISE FROM TOP: RADISH BUTTER (PAGE 82), LEE BROS. SHRIMP PÂTÉ (PAGE 60), AND BUTTERMILK FRESH CHEESE (PAGE 93)

F reddie's Crab Shack & Soul Food was a restaurant on Meeting Street in Charleston, opposite the Interstate 26 on-ramp, that closed, much to our dismay, in 2008. You couldn't miss the hand-painted signs at the edge of the parking lot that read, "Fried Crab," "Garlic Crab," and, when muscadine grapes were in season, "Bull Grape."

Freddie's fried crab was a bit of a marvel—whole hard-shell blue crabs battered and dropped in a fryer. As you picked and ate the crabs, you simply sucked the spiced breading off the shells. Just as messily impressive, we think, and yet more winning was Freddie's garlic crab: whole blue crabs tossed in a garlic powder hot sauce.

In our riff on Freddie's recipe, we take a few liberties: we clean and split the crabs so they're easier to serve and eat; we use fresh minced garlic in our chile sauce; and we serve them over a bed of watercress. Set down a plate of these during cocktail hour with a stack of clean kitchen towels at the ready, or serve them family-style at the table, as an appetizer. The cress, which gets soppy with the sauce as the platter rounds the table, provides a bitter-fresh counterpoint to the crabs' richness.

6 live blue crabs	½ teaspoon crushed dried red chile flakes	I bunch watercress, other peppery cress, arugula, or frisée (4 to 5 ounces)
6 tablespoons (¾ stick) unsalted butter	½ cup Texas Pete or other red hot sauce	Roughly chopped scallions or chives, for garnish (optional)
3 cloves garlic, minced	½ teaspoon cornstarch	

Fill an 8-quart stockpot two-thirds full of water and bring it to a boil over high heat. Transfer the crabs to the pot one by one, picking up each with tongs (approach them from the back of their carapaces) and submersing it in the water. Cook until their shells turn bright orange, about 2 minutes after the last crab goes in the pot. Transfer the crabs to a colander set in the sink, and run cold water over them. When they are cool enough to handle, remove the face of each crab (the strip on the front that encompasses the eyes and the mouth) using kitchen scissors. Then slip your thumb in the gap created between the top and bottom shells and pull off the top shell, exposing the feathery gills. Discard the top shell and the gills. (If you find any orange crab roe in there, reserve it and add it to the

(recipe continues)

sauté pan with the garlic and chile flakes in the next step.) Turn the crab over and slide the tip of a knife beneath the spot where the cape of the shell tapers to a point; lift the bottom shell off and discard it. Crack each crab in two down the middle. Cleaning the crabs will take about 10 minutes.

2 In a large sauté pan, melt the butter over medium heat until frothy. Add the garlic and chile flakes. Cook, stirring them around the pan, until the garlic is translucent and very fragrant, about 4 minutes. Add the hot sauce and cornstarch, whisk the contents of the pan to combine completely, and cook until the sauce just begins to bubble, about 2 minutes. Add the crabs to the pan and continue, turning them with tongs or a wooden spoon until all the crabs are evenly coated with the sauce. Cover, and cook just until the crabs are warmed through, about 3 minutes. Remove from the heat.

3 Garland a serving platter with the cress, leaving space in the center for the crabs. With tongs, transfer the crabs to the platter and pile them in a mound. If the remaining sauce in the pan has broken at all, whisk it until it's emulsified again, and then pour the sauce over the crabs. Scatter scallions on top, if desired.

SKILLET-ROASTED QUAIL WITH WILTED SPINACH

serves 4 · TIME: 10 minutes marination, 25 minutes cooking

Quail are small, delicate game birds in the pheasant family that make a superb first course or an impressive lunch with a slice of buttered toast. In this recipe, the quail are marinated, seared in a skillet, then oven-roasted; their marinade is repurposed as a glaze during roasting and then transformed into the warm dressing that wilts the greens and gives them a zippy ginger flavor.

This is a super-hip dish that doesn't take much time. In fact, purchasing the birds may be your biggest challenge. If you live in hunt country, you probably experience the same swings of plenitude and scarcity that we do: during the season, it seems like everyone's looking to give them away; at other times nobody's gifting, and you have to buy them from an upscale butcher. This last option tends to be costlier, but it isn't all bad, because you can ask the butcher to butterfly them (cut out the backbone so they lie flat in the skillet) and trim the legs for you.

One 3-ounce piece of fresh ginger, peeled	1 teaspoon kosher salt, plus more to taste	¼ teaspoon freshly ground black pepper
4 quail (about 1¾ pounds total)	1 tablespoon honey, sorghum syrup, or summer berry preserves	2 teaspoons canola oil
½ cup chicken broth		8 ounces fresh baby spinach or your favorite salad greens
¼ cup white wine vinegar	¾ teaspoon cornstarch	
¼ cup olive oil		

1 Grate the ginger onto a cutting board, using a ginger grater or a Microplane. Gather up the grated ginger and place it in a mound in the middle of a double thickness of paper towel. Pick up the corners of the paper towel and gently press the grated ginger over a small bowl to release the juice; you should have about 2 tablespoons ginger juice. Set it aside.

2 Heat the oven to 425°F.

3 Using kitchen shears or a chef's knife, cut the backbone out of the quail, and then cut off the feet if necessary. Discard any organs. Put the quail in a medium bowl or a gallon-size locking food storage bag. In a small bowl, whisk together the broth, reserved ginger juice, vinegar, olive oil, and ½ teaspoon of the salt. Pour the marinade over the quail, keeping the

(recipe continues)

empty marinade bowl at hand (you need not clean it). Add the honey and cornstarch to the empty marinade bowl, and keep it close by. Let the quail marinate for 10 minutes.

4 Take the birds from the marinade, shaking off any excess, and season the birds on both sides with the remaining ½ teaspoon salt and the black pepper. Pour the marinade into a small saucepan, bring it to a boil, and maintain a hard boil until the liquid has reduced by half, about 3 minutes. Add 2 tablespoons of this liquid to the bowl containing the honey and cornstarch, whisk them together to make a glaze, and reserve.

5 Pour the canola oil into a large cast-iron skillet and heat it over high heat until the oil smokes. Add the birds, breast side down (in batches if your skillet isn't large enough), and sear them until their skin is nicely golden brown, 3 to 4 minutes. Then flip them so the breast is facing up, spoon the glaze liberally over their breasts, and transfer the skillet to the oven. Roast until the quail are cooked through, about 5 minutes. (If you had to sear them in batches, gather the birds in the same pan; it's fine if they overlap a bit when they go in the oven.) Baste the birds with pan drippings.

6 Place the spinach in a medium bowl. Drizzle ⅓ cup of the reduced warm marinade over the greens, and toss until they are evenly coated and softened. Add more liquid to taste, but avoid overdressing the greens. Divide the spinach among 4 plates and top each mound with 1 warm quail. Serve immediately.

WEST INDIES SALAD

serves 4 as an appetizer or 8 as a cocktail-hour snack
TIME: 5 minutes preparation, I hour marination

As sure as "beignet" says New Orleans or "she-crab soup" says Charleston, "West Indies Salad" says Mobile, Alabama, because it was there that William Bayley, chef-proprietor of Bayley's Corner, invented this simple yet impressive marinated crab salad in 1947. Served in a butter lettuce cup, or over fresh greens, it's as swell an appetizer as you could serve your in-laws; on a plate, with a passel of saltines, it's a crab dip for a rowdier gathering.

8 ounces fresh crab claw meat (not canned; about 1½ cups)

I medium sweet onion, finely diced (about ¾ cup)

Kosher salt and freshly ground black pepper

¼ cup champagne vinegar, white wine vinegar, or distilled white vinegar

¼ cup vegetable or peanut oil

6 ounces (about 6 cups) tender salad greens, such as butter lettuce, green leaf lettuce, arugula, lolla rossa, dandelion greens, or any mixture thereof

I tablespoon minced fresh tarragon (leaves from 4 to 6 stems)

Saltines or other water crackers (optional)

1 In a medium bowl, mix the crab and the onion, tossing gently with a fork until evenly combined. Season to taste with salt and black pepper.

2 In a small bowl, whisk the vinegar with the vegetable oil and ¼ cup cold water until the mixture is thoroughly emulsified. Pour the dressing over the crab and onion mixture, cover with plastic wrap, and let marinate in the refrigerator for 1 hour.

3 Put the salad greens in a large salad bowl. Using a fine-mesh strainer, strain the marinated crab and onion mixture over the greens. Return the crab salad to the bowl it marinated in, add the tarragon, and toss gently with a fork until the tarragon is evenly distributed throughout. Toss the salad greens in the bowl until the leaves are evenly coated with the dressing.

4 Divide the dressed salad greens evenly among 4 small bowls or plates. Mound a quarter of the crab-salad mixture in the center of each bowl. Serve immediately, with saltines if desired.

NOTE We use crab claw meat because it's an inexpensive grade of crabmeat with rich crab flavor and because it holds up well when marinated. But if you prefer higher-class lump crabmeat, this dish won't suffer for it!

CLAMS WITH SWEET POTATO, SMOKED SAUSAGE, AND WATERCRESS

serves 4 as a small plate or 2 as a main dish
TIME: 10 minutes preparation, 20 minutes cooking

Where we're from, oysters get more attention than clams do, and we're guessing it's because they're simply easier to see. Hard-shell clams develop beneath the mud, whereas oysters grow up and out of the mud banks in clusters, so you just can't miss them after the tide's gone out. But there is, in fact, a sizable commercial trade in hard-shell clams from South Carolina, even if they tend to get shipped to large wholesale markets in Baltimore, New York, and Boston.

Away from the commercial clam beds, the bivalves are rarely molested by recreational fishermen, so they tend to grow very large, the size of a fist, with meats as large as hamburgers. These large clams—or any clams 3½ inches across or larger, called chowders—are not as desirable as smaller cherrystones (about 2½ inches across) or the even more valuable 1½-inch littlenecks, which are tender, sweet, and easy to eat. Still, if we're gathering oysters for a roast and we find a few chowder clams, we're always thrilled to roast them up the same way we do our oysters: on a hot griddle over a wood fire with nothing more than a drop of pepper vinegar.

This clam recipe has a few more elements than that, but it's even simpler than roasting because there's no wood to gather and no fire to build. And the synergy of briny clam, smoky sausage, soft sweet potato, and crunchy-bitter watercress is otherworldly; it has become as popular a weeknight dish on our dinner table as our Skirt Steak with Parsley Sauce (page 171). Every bite, you think: This is just *way* too easy to be this satisfying.

---

3 ounces smoked sausage, such as Cajun andouille, Polish kielbasa, or cured (fully cooked) chorizo, sliced thinly or diced

2 cups full-flavored dry white wine, such as unoaked Chardonnay, Grüner Veltliner, or Viognier

½ teaspoon kosher salt

¾ pound sweet potatoes, peeled and cut into ½-inch dice (about 3 cups)

24 littleneck clams, or 16 cherrystone clams (see Clam Shopping Notes, page 58)

1 bunch watercress (4 to 5 ounces), stems trimmed

(recipe continues)

1   In a 3-quart Dutch oven or saucepan, sauté the sausage over medium-high heat, stirring occasionally, until the pieces are just beginning to brown and have rendered their fat, 5 to 6 minutes. Using a slotted spoon, transfer about half the sausage pieces to a double thickness of paper towel to drain. Leave the rest in the pan.

2   Add 2 cups water, the wine, and the salt, cover, and bring to a boil. Then add the sweet potatoes, and when the liquid returns to a boil, continue to cook for 3 minutes. Add the clams, and continue to cook until all the clams have opened and the sweet potatoes are tender, 6 to 8 minutes. Discard any clams that don't open.

garnish it bright
...
With wedges of lemon.

3   Arrange a tangle of watercress (about 2 sprigs) in the bottom of each of 4 soup bowls. Divide the clams, sweet potatoes, sausage, and broth evenly among the bowls, and garnish with the reserved sausage and another tangle of watercress. Serve immediately.

VARIATION

hot and spicy clams with sweet potato, smoked sausage, and watercress If you enjoy the heat of dried red chiles and the aromatic twinge of garlic, add ½ teaspoon crushed dried red chile flakes and 3 cloves chopped fresh garlic to the pot just after transferring half the sausage from the pot to the paper towel. Stir the garlic and crushed chile around in the sausage fat until the garlic is translucent and golden (but not brown)— about 30 seconds—before adding the liquids and salt.

clam shopping notes ... When buying raw clams, avoid any clam whose shell has opened or looks damaged. If your fish market selects your clams for you, be sure the fishmonger chooses them carefully, checking for quality—and not simply with the eyes, either; a top-quality purveyor will "knock" the clams together lightly as he selects them, listening for the higher, hollow tone that indicates the clam has lost its liquid and should be discarded.

CHEESE RELISH

Washington, D.C., Matt's birthplace, isn't well regarded for its food traditions, but our ears perked up when former Senate Majority Leader Howard Baker Jr.'s niece, Barbara Harr, told us about his favorite sandwich spread, an unusual pimento cheese variant and D.C. specialty known as "cheese relish." Where the pimento cheese we know and love contains cheddar and roasted red peppers, this spread has Swiss cheese and yellow banana peppers, with capers mixed in. We couldn't locate an original source (please alert us if you know more), so we developed this formula, which has the Swiss cheese flavor we adore plus the unique soft heat of banana peppers, in equal balance, punctuated by salty capers. It tastes best when prepared a day before serving, so the flavors have time to marinate in the fridge. Try it spread on crackers as a snack, or in a grilled sandwich, served with a glass of dry Riesling.

10 ounces Swiss cheese, finely grated (about 3½ cups)	¼ teaspoon freshly ground black pepper	2 tablespoons minced fresh chives
One 12-ounce jar banana peppers (hot if available), drained and minced	¼ teaspoon crushed dried red chile flakes	2 tablespoons drained capers, soaked in fresh water for 1 minute and then drained again
3 tablespoons sour cream	¼ teaspoon kosher salt	

With a spatula, combine all the ingredients together in a large mixing bowl until evenly blended. Cover and refrigerate for 2 hours or overnight.

LEE BROS. SHRIMP PÂTÉ

serves 12 as a cocktail-hour snack • TIME: 10 minutes preparation, 12 minutes cooking

We call our riff on the classic Charleston shrimp paste "Shrimp Pâté" simply because the word "paste" doesn't sound appetizing. Call it what you wish, shrimp paste is a recipe prized as much for versatility as for flavor: it is served in tea sandwiches in the afternoon, spread on crackers or celery sticks at the cocktail hour, and is also wonderful the following morning, stirred into a bowl of stone-ground grits. Blanche Rhett's *Two Hundred Years of Charleston Cooking,* one of the city's seminal cookbooks, contains three different recipes for shrimp paste, each of which has a different approach to flavoring: one is studded with diced bell pepper and onion, another is spiced with nutmeg, and one couldn't be simpler: butter, shrimp, and salt. But all three recipes call for baking the paste until it browns.

We aimed to simplify things without compromising an ounce on the flavor. We did away with the baking, and we dialed back the quantity of sherry that usually finds its way into shrimp paste because we think that even the mellowest fortified wine can overpower the delicate sweetness of the shrimp. We tried some flights of fancy—ginger and lemon zest—which worked out okay, but in the end we returned, again, to simplicity. This mixture of steamed fresh shrimp, unsalted butter, and sherry needs nothing more than a touch of lemon juice, salt, and freshly ground black pepper.

1 pound headless large shell-on shrimp (26 to 30 per pound; see Shrimp Shopping Notes, page 63) 1¼ teaspoons kosher salt, plus more to taste	8 tablespoons (1 stick) unsalted butter, cut into pieces, at room temperature 1½ tablespoons fresh lemon juice, plus more to taste 1½ tablespoons dry sherry	½ teaspoon freshly ground black pepper, plus more to taste Crackers, celery sticks, or toasted baguette slices, for serving

1. Peel the shrimp, discarding the shells, and devein them (see Notes on Deveining Shrimp, opposite). Pour 3 cups water into a medium saucepan, add 1 teaspoon of the salt, and bring to a boil over high heat. Remove the pan from the heat, add the shrimp, and cook (off the heat) until bright pink, about 1 minute. Drain the shrimp and run them under cold running water to cool completely. Agitate the strainer to shake any excess water from the shrimp, and pat them dry with a paper towel.

2   Put the shrimp in the bowl of a food processor and add the remaining
    ¼ teaspoon salt, the butter, lemon juice, sherry, and black pepper. Pulse
    until the mixture becomes a fine-textured spread, about ten 5-second
    pulses. Season to taste with lemon juice, salt, and black pepper, if
    necessary, pulsing again to incorporate.

3   Transfer the pâté to a large ramekin or a small bowl, pat plastic wrap
    directly on the surface to prevent oxidation, and refrigerate for no more
    than 2 days.

4   Remove the pâté from the refrigerator 10 minutes before serving, to let it
    soften. Serve as a spread with crackers, celery sticks, or toasted baguette
    slices.

notes on deveining shrimp ··· The "vein" of a shrimp is
its digestive tract, which is flavorless, harmless to eat, and doesn't pro-
nouncedly affect its flavor or its texture; still, some eaters detect a certain
grittiness when it hasn't been removed. Whether or not you devein shrimp is
a matter of personal preference. We do it when presentation is paramount
and, in the case of this shrimp pâté, it is. You can devein raw shrimp with
the shell on or off, but larger shrimp with tough shells may require shelling
first. Either way, the technique is the same: hold the shrimp between your
thumb and forefinger one-third of an inch behind where the head was cut
off. Place the tip of a sharp paring knife with the blade facing up in the
slight indentation at the top of the shrimp body (which may or may not have
a dark spot of vein marking it), and push the blade toward the tail, making a
shallow incision the length of the shrimp's back. This will expose the dark
vein, which you can then remove with the tip of a paring knife.

shrimp shopping notes ⋯ In our books, shrimp always appear in the ingredients list as "headless shrimp, shells on." That's because fish markets and supermarkets commonly sell fresh shrimp as such, so finding them is easy. Also, leaving the shells on until you're ready to use the shrimp keeps them from losing their natural moisture, thus retaining both flavor and texture. And the shrimp shells themselves bear a bounty of flavor, so we often use them to make shrimp broth.

Buy shrimp only according to the count per pound, and never by descriptions such as "large" or "medium." We've found these descriptions to fluctuate from shop to shop. A good fish market will always know the count per pound of each variety of shrimp it offers. These are average numbers, of course, which is why they are always expressed as a range. If the market does not know the piece-per-pound count, ask them to place a dozen or so on a scale to determine how much they weigh. The size we favor for most of our recipes—unless specified otherwise—is 26 to 30 shrimp per pound, which is generally considered "large." Don't be tempted to buy jumbo shrimp if large or even medium are equally fresh. We find jumbos can be rubbery on the outside by the time the inside is cooked through, so unless the jumbos are the freshest variety in your market, go for "large" (26–30/pound) instead.

Wherever you shop for fish, demand fresh shrimp caught wild in American waters. Much of the shrimp sold in American markets comes from farms on the far side of the Pacific Ocean, where it is frozen and then shipped to wholesale markets in the United States. These shrimp are damaged by their long journey, and you can often tell simply by looking at them: the meat will be flaking from freezer burn, the shells turning opaque and falling off. This severely affects the flavor, texture, and the appearance of your dish. And while it goes without saying that when you encounter several varieties of shrimp at the market, you should buy the shrimp that looks freshest, we've yet to find a market whose farmed Asian shrimp are fresher or tastier than their wild American shrimp.

SHRIMP

→

G.A. MAGWOOD & SONS

FRESH SHRIMP

OPEN Fresh
Local SHRIMP

Magwood
Seafood

JADE SHRIMP COCKTAIL

serves 4 · TIME: 15 minutes preparation, 15 minutes refrigeration

We're always seeking new recipes to flatter the sparklingly fresh local shrimp we buy in South Carolina, at docks in Shem Creek and Rockville. Recently we became restless with the ketchupy sauce typically served with shrimp cocktail, and decided to spin it in a green direction, using tart green tomatoes and tomatillos. The avocado and cayenne in this recipe nudge our cocktail sauce toward a guacamole, but stop just shy. It's tropically inclined but still familiar, an intriguing new take on an old favorite.

4½ teaspoons kosher salt, plus more to taste

1 teaspoon ground cayenne pepper

1 pound headless large shell-on shrimp (26 to 30 per pound; see Notes on Deveining Shrimp, page 61, and Shrimp Shopping Notes, page 63)

1 pound tomatillos (husks removed) or green tomatoes, cored and quartered

2 scallions, green tops only

1 ripe avocado, halved, pitted, and peeled (see page 134)

2 tablespoons prepared horseradish, drained

1 teaspoon honey

2 tablespoons fresh lemon juice

Freshly ground black pepper

1   Bring 2 quarts water, 2 teaspoons of the salt, and the cayenne pepper to a boil in a 4- to 6-quart pot. Remove from the heat, add the shrimp, and cook (off the heat) for 1 minute, until they're bright pink-orange and slightly firm. Drain, and rinse with cold water to keep the shrimp from cooking further and to make peeling easier. Peel the shrimp, leaving the tails on for grasping (this takes about 8 minutes). Refrigerate the shrimp for 15 minutes to cool them further.

2   While the shrimp are chilling, place the tomatillos in a food processor and pulse to form a smooth puree. Drain the puree through a medium-mesh strainer, reserving the strained tomatillo water. Return the puree from the strainer to the food processor (you need not wash the bowl), and add the scallion tops, avocado, horseradish, honey, lemon juice, remaining 2½ teaspoons salt, and 1 tablespoon of the reserved tomatillo water. Process to a smooth puree. Season to taste with salt and black pepper, and adjust the consistency of the sauce as needed with more of the reserved tomatillo water. Transfer the sauce to a ramekin or a small serving bowl. (The sauce will keep for 3 days in the refrigerator.)

3   Serve the chilled shrimp with the dipping sauce.

8 SIMPLE FRESH PICKLES

We love pickles so much that in our first cookbook, we devoted an entire chapter—13 recipes spanning 38 pages—to them. Since that time, we've only become more flat-out crazy for pickles, making them more frequently than ever—a few quarts a week. We've found that the pickles themselves have moved closer to the center of the plate, so to speak, in our eating lives. We serve them often as a side dish—almost like a marinated salad, but with a turbo kick—with fried foods, with grilled fish, chicken, beef, or pork, with anything especially meaty or charry. In fact, we were tempted to put these recipes in the "Salads and Cold Sides" chapter, but we find we eat them just as often for snacking before the meal. When guests are over for drinks, nothing's easier than setting out a platter of delights straight from the fridge: an assortment of fresh pickles, a Buttermilk Fresh Cheese (page 93) with crackers or bread, and paper-thin slices of country ham.

We've also found that the more we pickle, the more laid-back our technique has become. Here's what we do: (1) Pack the veggies in a quart-size vessel, (2) heat up the brine and pour it over them, (3) let the pickles cool to room temperature and then refrigerate further to chill. That's all. Overnight marination in the fridge is optimal, but in most of these pickle recipes, the veggies (or fruit) are cut thin, so after an hour in the fridge, they're ready to go. And go they do: these are not pickles to store on a shelf in the garage so that next spring somebody can find the dusty jar while looking for a bottle of motor oil for the Buick. These are pickles you keep at the front of your fridge, so you can work their deliciousness into as many meals as possible.

CARROT PICKLES WITH SHALLOTS AND DILL

makes 1 quart · TIME: 10 minutes preparation, 30 minutes cooling, 1 hour refrigeration

Crunchy and cool, these carrot pickles have a mellow natural sweetness. If you can't find fresh dill, substitute fresh cilantro or the Mexican herb epazote for an aromatic, caraway-like zip. Superb on sandwiches and tucked into tacos.

1½ pounds carrots, trimmed and peeled, sliced on the bias ⅛ inch thick

8 ounces shallots (about 2 large shallots), thinly sliced

6 sprigs fresh dill, cilantro, or epazote

1 cup distilled white vinegar or white wine vinegar

4 cloves garlic, crushed and peeled

2 teaspoons kosher salt

1 teaspoon sugar

½ teaspoon celery seeds

2 teaspoons whole black peppercorns

Combine the carrots, shallots, and dill in a quart-size glass container with a lid. In a small saucepan, combine 1 cup water with the vinegar, garlic, salt, sugar, celery seeds, and peppercorns, and heat until it simmers. Pour the brine over the veggies, cover loosely, and let cool to room temperature. Seal the container and chill in the refrigerator for 1 hour before serving. The pickles will keep in the refrigerator for about 2 weeks.

WATERMELON AND ONION PICKLES

makes 1 quart · TIME: 10 minutes preparation, 1 hour refrigeration

Not your mama's watermelon rind pickles! We make these sweet-and-sours with bright red watermelon flesh, cutting it up into small tiles and pickling it along with sweet onion and basil. Serve a side of these with take-out fried chicken and you've got a meal with down-home flavor. With piping hot fried oysters, these pickles are dynamite!

One 2½-pound piece underripe or ripe fresh watermelon, cut into 1-x-1-x-⅓-inch "tiles" (1 scant quart)

1 large (8-ounce) sweet onion, sliced into thin rings

2 sprigs fresh basil or flat-leaf parsley (optional)

½ cup white wine vinegar

½ teaspoon kosher salt

⅛ teaspoon crushed dried red chile flakes

Layer the watermelon, onion, and basil in a quart-size glass container with a lid. Pour 1⅓ cups water and the vinegar into a small bowl, add the salt and the chile flakes, and stir until the salt dissolves. Pour it over the fruit, cover, and chill for 1 hour in the refrigerator before serving. The pickles will keep in the refrigerator for about 1 week.

PICKLED GRAPES WITH ROSEMARY AND CHILES

makes 1½ quarts · TIME: 10 minutes preparation, 30 minutes cooling, 1 hour refrigeration

Pickled grapes look a lot like olives, and we use them a lot like olives, too, tossing them in cold salads or just serving them in a ramekin as a cocktail nibble, with toothpicks (no dish for pits required!). Their playful sweet-sour flavor, their crispness, and their gentle chile heat make them super-addictive.

6 cups stemmed mixed red and green seedless grapes (about 2 pounds)	2 tablespoons kosher salt	Leaves from 1 four-inch sprig rosemary
	2 teaspoons sugar	½ teaspoon crushed dried red chile flakes
2 cups distilled white vinegar or white wine vinegar	3 cloves garlic, crushed and peeled	

Pack the grapes into 3 pint-size glass containers with lids. Pour the vinegar and 1 cup water into a saucepan, set it over medium-high heat, and add the salt, sugar, garlic, rosemary, and chile flakes. When the mixture starts to simmer, remove the pan from the heat and divide the hot brine among the pints of grapes. Cover loosely and let cool to room temperature. Cover tightly and chill in the refrigerator for about 1 hour before serving. The pickles will keep in the refrigerator for about 2 weeks.

ZUCCHINI AND ONION PICKLES

makes 1 quart • TIME: 10 minutes preparation, 30 minutes cooling, 1 hour refrigeration

We're always looking to transform inexpensive stalwarts of the produce section into something astounding. Here we combine yellow summer squash and green zucchini for the appealing mixture of color, but you can use either color alone if you prefer a more monochromatic look, or if one variety is less than fresh in the market the day you shop.

1 pound green zucchini and/or yellow squash (about 2 medium), sliced on the bias ⅛ inch thick

1 large (8-ounce) white onion, sliced into thin rings

1 cup distilled white vinegar or white wine vinegar

3 large cloves garlic, crushed and peeled

2 teaspoons kosher salt

1 teaspoon sugar

1 teaspoon whole black peppercorns

Layer the zucchini, squash, and onion in a quart-size glass container with a lid. Pour 1 cup water and the vinegar into a small saucepan, set it over medium-high heat, and add the garlic, salt, sugar, and peppercorns. When it starts to simmer, remove the pan from the heat and pour the brine over the vegetables. Cover loosely and let cool to room temperature. Seal the container and chill in the refrigerator for 1 hour before serving. The pickles will keep in the refrigerator for about 2 weeks.

FROM LEFT TO RIGHT: PICKLED GRAPES WITH ROSEMARY AND CHILES (PAGE 73), WATERMELON AND ONION PICKLES (PAGE 71), AND ZUCCHINI AND ONION PICKLES

RADISH PICKLES

makes 1 quart • TIME: 10 minutes preparation, 30 minutes cooling, 1 hour refrigeration

Peppery, radiant-red radishes make beautiful and sublime pickles that you're unlikely to find anywhere else. Look for bright, unblemished radishes.

2 pounds round red radishes, such as Cherry Belles or Champions, trimmed and sliced on the bias ⅛ inch thick	1 cup distilled white vinegar or white wine vinegar 4 cloves garlic, crushed and peeled 2 teaspoons kosher salt	1 teaspoon sugar ⅛ teaspoon ground turmeric (optional) 1 teaspoon whole black peppercorns

Layer the radishes in a quart-size glass container with a lid. Pour the vinegar and 1 cup water into a small saucepan, set it over medium-high heat, and add the garlic, salt, sugar, turmeric, and peppercorns. When the mixture starts to simmer, remove the pan from the heat and pour the brine over the radishes. Cover loosely and let cool to room temperature. Then seal the container tightly and chill in the refrigerator for 1 hour or more before serving. The pickles will keep in the refrigerator for about 2 weeks.

GINGERED BEET PICKLES

makes 1 quart • TIME: 10 minutes preparation, 30 minutes cooling, 1 hour refrigeration

Gingered beets are a classic southern side dish that can be served warm or cold. But this brilliant pairing also makes a pickle that's as easy to eat as it is likely to stain your seersucker.

One 2-inch piece fresh ginger, peeled and sliced into about 8 thin disks (¼ cup)	1 cup distilled white vinegar 2 teaspoons kosher salt	1 teaspoon sugar 1¼ pounds red beets, peeled and very thinly sliced

Pour 1 cup water into a medium saucepan over medium-high heat, and add the ginger, vinegar, salt, and sugar. When the brine simmers, add the beets, and when it returns to a simmer, continue to cook for 4 minutes. Remove the pan from the heat, cover loosely, and let cool to room temperature. Transfer to a quart-size glass container with a lid, and seal tightly. Chill further in the refrigerator for 1 hour or until ready to serve. The pickles will keep in the refrigerator for about 2 weeks.

LEMON AND CUCUMBER PICKLES

makes 1 quart · TIME: 10 minutes preparation, 30 minutes cooling, 1 hour refrigeration

The combination of dill with cucumber pickles is rote and expected. Pairing the cucumbers with lemon, however, is surprisingly delicious. Burgers and sandwiches get a nice bump when they're scattered with these thin disks.

1 pound Persian or Kirby cucumbers, trimmed (not peeled) and sliced on the bias ⅛ inch thick 1 large shallot, thinly sliced	4 cloves garlic, crushed and peeled ½ cup distilled white vinegar or white wine vinegar 1 cup fresh lemon juice (from 6 large lemons)	2½ teaspoons kosher salt 1½ teaspoons sugar 1 teaspoon whole black peppercorns

Put the cucumbers, shallots, and garlic in a quart-size glass container with a lid. Pour the vinegar, lemon juice, and ½ cup water into a saucepan, set it over medium-high heat, and add the salt, sugar, and peppercorns. When the mixture starts to simmer, remove the pan from the heat and pour the brine over the cucumbers. Cover the container loosely and let cool to room temperature. Then seal it tightly and chill in the refrigerator for about 1 hour before serving. The pickles will keep in the refrigerator for about 2 weeks.

GREEN TOMATO AND ONION PICKLES

makes 1 quart · TIME: 10 minutes preparation, 30 minutes cooling, 1 hour refrigeration

Green tomatoes practically pickle themselves, they're so crisp and tart. We add a little ginger to ours, and the vinegary brine brings out their strange savory character. These pickles are excellent fried (see variation below).

12 ounces green tomatoes, very thinly sliced	One 2-inch piece fresh ginger, peeled and sliced into about 8 thin disks	2 teaspoons kosher salt
1 large white onion, sliced into thin rings	1 cup distilled white vinegar, white wine vinegar, or apple cider vinegar	1 teaspoon sugar

Layer the green tomatoes, onion rings, and ginger in a quart-size glass container with a lid. Pour 1 cup water and the vinegar into a small saucepan, add the salt and sugar, and bring to a boil. Pour the brine over the vegetables, cover loosely, and let cool to room temperature. Seal the container tightly and chill in the refrigerator for 1 hour before serving. The pickles will keep in the refrigerator for about 2 weeks.

VARIATION

fried green tomato and onion pickles Whoever first fried pickles was onto something great, and if you've never tried it, you should: crispy cornmeal crust around a tart, snappy pickle is a singular taste sensation. Since fried green tomatoes are a staple of the southern diet, it makes sense to fry green tomato pickles. It's easy, too.

1   Heat 2 cups of peanut oil in a large skillet to 375°F.

2   Dredge 1 quart of green tomato and onion pickles in a mixture of ½ cup all-purpose flour, 3 tablespoons fine stone-ground cornmeal, 1 tablespoon dry bread crumbs, 2 teaspoons table salt, and 1½ teaspoons coarsely ground black pepper.

3   Fry the dredged pickles in batches, turning them as they become golden, until they're golden brown all over, about 2 minutes per side. Serve in butcher-paper cones with fried oysters as a snack.

OYSTER COCKTAILS

We love the salty, meaty oysters we harvest from local waters around Charleston, and we typically roast them over an open fire, shuck 'em, and slurp 'em down. Nothing fancy. When the globe-trotting food maven Anthony Bourdain recently came to town looking to find out how locals eat, we took him to meet our friend Sam Van Norte, a roaster par excellence who harvests them from the creek that runs through his farm on Edisto Island. Bourdain said it best to the camera when he downed his first oyster: "Delicious! Good oysters need no preparation."

We couldn't agree more. But on some occasions, we're inclined to dress up our oysters, marinating them in a cocktail of sweet, sour, and aromatic elements that highlights their bracing brininess. Here are two of our favorite oyster cocktails. Serve them on a leaf of butter lettuce in stainless steel sundae cups, with a few saltines or endive leaves for scooping up the cocktail.

oyster shopping notes ··· Most fishmongers offer a couple varieties of oysters in the shell for shucking at home, and many will shuck the oysters for you for a $2 surcharge on the price of a dozen—a great value in our estimation. But unless you're lucky enough to live in a coastal place like Charleston, the price of a dozen oysters in the shell may itself be prohibitive. Not to worry: most independent fish markets and the fish counters of larger grocery stores offer less expensive half-pint or pint-size plastic tubs of shucked oysters in their liquor. Packed in Washington State, Virginia, Maryland, Louisiana, North Carolina, or Florida, these oysters are mostly used in cooked preparations, but we often use them raw for our oyster cocktails, and we've never once been disappointed by their quality or freshness. Most containers are marked with a packing date and a use-by date, but as with any shellfish, if you're concerned, don't hesitate to ask your fishmonger if they're fresh enough to consume raw. And always buy jars labeled "selects" if possible, because they tend to be more uniformly sized. One caveat: to our taste, packed oysters rarely have enough brine, because the packers almost always soak them in fresh water to plump them up and bring down the salt content. Fortunately, that can be easily remedied with several pinches of kosher salt to taste (we commonly use a teaspoon per pint). At about $10 a pint (24 to 36 oysters, depending on their size), they're one of America's great seafood bargains. And if you're at all cringy about eating these oysters raw, simply heat them in their liquor in a skillet or sauté pan until their edges curl, and then proceed with the cocktail recipes.

OYSTER COCKTAIL NO. I

lemon, fiery habanero, and parsley

serves 4 • TIME: 10 minutes preparation, 30 minutes resting

1½ cups freshly shucked oysters with their liquor (about 16 pieces)

1 red habanero chile, seeded and minced (1 tablespoon)

1 large lemon, segmented (see Segmenting Citrus, page 130)

¼ cup finely chopped fresh flat-leaf parsley

3 tablespoons white wine vinegar

3 tablespoons dry white wine

1 teaspoon kosher salt

2 tablespoons extra-virgin olive oil

Freshly ground black pepper

---

1   Strain the liquor from the oysters and discard all but 2 tablespoons. Pour the oysters and the reserved liquor into a medium bowl. Add the chile, lemon, parsley, vinegar, white wine, and salt, and toss gently to combine. Cover and let rest in the refrigerator for at least 30 minutes (but not more than a day) to let the flavors meld before serving.

2   To serve, divide the oyster mixture among small bowls. Drizzle each serving with 1½ teaspoons of the oil, grind a bit of fresh black pepper over them, and serve with a small spoon.

OYSTER COCKTAIL NO. 2

tart apple, lime, and jalapeño

serves 4 • TIME: 10 minutes preparation, 30 minutes resting

1½ cups freshly shucked oysters with their liquor (about 16 pieces)

1 medium jalapeño chile, seeded and very finely diced (2 tablespoons)

1 lime, segmented (see Segmenting Citrus, page 130)

¼ cup finely chopped scallions (white and green parts)

2 tablespoons white wine vinegar

½ Granny Smith apple, peeled, cored, and cut into matchsticks

1 teaspoon kosher salt

2 tablespoons extra-virgin olive oil

Freshly ground black pepper

1 Strain the liquor from the oysters and discard all but 2 tablespoons. Pour the oysters and the reserved liquor into a medium bowl. Add the chile, lime, scallions, vinegar, apple, and salt, and toss gently to combine. Cover and let rest in the refrigerator for at least 30 minutes (but not more than a day) to let the flavors meld before serving.

2 To serve, divide the oyster mixture among small bowls or wineglasses. Drizzle each serving with 1½ teaspoons of the oil, grind a bit of fresh black pepper over them, and serve with a small spoon.

RADISH BUTTER

serves 6 · TIME: 10 minutes

This simple veggie spread will knock you out first with its speckled-magenta beauty. Then you'll be impressed by how it synthesizes the old-school delight of peppery, cool radishes from the garden, dabbed with a dot of good butter and a pinch of salt. Spread it on rye toast points, unsalted crackers, celery sticks, endive leaves, or crunchy romaine hearts.

We got the idea for radish butter from our Nashville friend Mindy Merrell, the co-author, with her guy, R. B. Quinn, of *Cheater BBQ: Barbecue Anytime, Anywhere, in Any Weather.* For folks who call themselves "cheater chefs," they sure don't skimp on anything, and they come up with ideas that are simple and original and damned delicious. We think you'll agree "clever chefs" is more like it.

½ pound round red radishes, trimmed, at room temperature	¼ teaspoon kosher salt, or ½ teaspoon Maldon salt	About 24 thinly sliced rye toast points, toasted slices of French bread, water crackers, 2-inch celery sticks, endive leaves, or romaine heart halves
6 tablespoons unsalted butter, completely softened	⅛ teaspoon freshly ground white or black pepper	

Put the radishes in the bowl of a food processor and pulse until the radish is chopped into very fine dice, four or five 3-second pulses. Transfer the contents to a length of cheesecloth or a double thickness of paper towels and wring out the excess liquid. Transfer to a medium bowl and add 4 tablespoons of the butter. With a rubber spatula, cream the radish and butter together, adding more butter 1 tablespoon at a time, until the mixture comes together in a smooth, pliable mass. Transfer the mixture to a 2-cup ramekin or bowl, sprinkle the salt and pepper over the top, and serve immediately. (The butter will keep, covered with plastic wrap, in the refrigerator for up to 2 days. Remove it from the refrigerator 15 minutes before serving to let it soften. Sprinkle the salt and freshly ground pepper over the radish butter before serving.)

SALT-AND-PEPPER SHRIMP

a tribute to 101 spring street

serves 4 as a snack or 2 as an appetizer with salad greens · TIME: 10 minutes

This recipe is about the best, quickest, and easiest treatment of great shrimp we know of—just salt, pepper, shell-on shrimp, and a sturdy aromatic seasoning leaf like bay or kaffir lime. At our first book party in Charleston, the fates were aligned. A friend in line to get her cookbook signed thrust a plastic Piggly-Wiggly grocery bag into Matt's hand. "This shrimp was caught last night—got it this morning at the docks." Another generous friend, a neighbor, brought a gift of kaffir lime leaves (used to season Thai curries) from her garden.

At the time our friend Will was renting an old falling-down Charleston house with a wide wooden porch suitable for dancing (it had some spring to it, and a chandelier). Once the official book event wrapped up, we marched everyone up to Will's porch for an after-party. When appetites surged later that evening, we looked around and remembered the bag of shrimp. Will doesn't keep much of anything in his pantry, but we didn't need a whole lot: a skillet, ground pepper, a scattering of salt. While we were at it, we threw in a few lime leaves to add some aromatic mojo to the operation and a splash of Budweiser at the last minute for good measure. We simply moved the skillet to the porch, and in a few moments it was empty. Shrimp that tiny, fresh, and tender don't require peeling, so people could pop them in the mouth as is. When we make this recipe with shrimp with thicker, tougher shells, of course we peel 'em; even so, pan-fried shrimp tails are among the most flavorful parts of the crustacean, and often crisp enough to eat. Serve with your favorite beer, or with pink bubbly.

¼ cup peanut oil

2 seasoning leaves, such as bay or kaffir lime, or ½ bulb lemongrass

1 pound headless large shell-on shrimp (26 to 30 per pound; see Notes on Deveining Shrimp, page 61, and Shrimp Shopping Notes, page 63)

2 teaspoons kosher salt

1 tablespoon freshly ground black pepper

A couple splashes of beer (optional)

1 Pour the oil into a large skillet set over medium-high heat. When it shimmers, add the bay leaves and the shrimp, and smooth them out in a single layer. Season the shrimp with 1 teaspoon of the salt and ½ tablespoon of the pepper, and cook for about 3 minutes, or until the shrimp shells begin to toast, releasing an intensely shrimpy aroma. Splash with the beer, if using, then use a slotted metal spatula to flip the shrimp over. Season them with the remaining 1 teaspoon salt and ½ tablespoon pepper, and cook for 2 minutes more.

2 Transfer the shrimp (using the same spatula) to a plate lined with paper towels and serve immediately, with paper towels (or napkins, if you prefer) and a bowl for the shells, if necessary.

SWEET POTATO AND OKRA FRITTERS WITH GARLIC BUTTERMILK DIP

serves 6 as a snack or 4 as an appetizer • TIME: 30 minutes resting, 24 minutes cooking

We don't care to let classic southern vegetables, like okra and sweet potatoes, live a life of predictability. They've performed centuries of solid duty as the third-best dish on the buffet line, boiled and seasoned and never quite given the full range of possibilities that American cooks offer to their kin, corn and tomatoes. We like to help such unsung heroes escape their traditional roles with recipes that are dramatically different in format (see Butterbean Mash, page 200) but true to the spirit of their flavor.

Rootsy sweet potatoes get to show off in this perfect appetizer, which relies on a matchup with okra to lend the fritters their spongy-crispy texture. Peanuts, in the form of peanut oil (expensive, but worth it), give the fritters that lusciousness we all crave. The cooling hit of a garlic buttermilk dip is essential to round it all out. Serve these as a cocktail-hour snack—use a fork and knife if you must; we use our hands—with a dry sparkling white wine, or as an appetizer.

FRITTER BATTER

1 pound sweet potatoes, peeled and coarsely grated on a box grater or in a food processor

2 teaspoons kosher salt, plus more to taste

6 ounces fresh okra, cut into ¼- to ⅓-inch-thick rounds (1⅔ cups)

½ cup finely chopped scallions (white and green parts)

½ teaspoon freshly ground black pepper

3 tablespoons dry bread crumbs

3 tablespoons sifted all-purpose flour

1 large egg, beaten

2 tablespoons half-and-half

GARLIC BUTTERMILK DIP

½ cup whole or lowfat buttermilk

½ cup sour cream

1 teaspoon kosher salt, or more to taste

½ large clove garlic, grated on a Microplane grater

3 cups peanut oil

1 Toss the grated sweet potatoes with 1 teaspoon of the salt in a large bowl, and let stand at room temperature for 15 minutes.

2 Wring the sweet potato dry by handfuls over the sink, and return them to the bowl. Add the okra, scallions, remaining 1 teaspoon salt, the pepper, bread crumbs, and flour, and toss until evenly combined. Add the egg and half-and-half, mix together, and let stand for 15 minutes at room temperature. Then beat the mixture with a wooden spoon or spatula for about a full minute until it's very sticky (in this regard, the okra is key).

3   Prepare the garlic buttermilk dip: In a medium bowl, whisk the butter-milk with the sour cream, salt, and garlic. Season to taste with more salt, if needed. Set the dip aside.

4   Set oven to warm (200°F), and place in it a baking pan or ovenproof platter lined with a double thickness of paper towels.

5   In a large heavy-bottomed pot, heat the oil to 365°F. Use a large serving spoon to shape the sweet potato mixture into fritters by scooping a rounded spoonful from the bowl, placing it on a clean baking sheet or cutting board, and lightly pressing down on the center of the mixture with the back of the spoon to flatten it before moving on to the next fritter. Gently roll each fritter into the hot oil with a slotted spoon or skimmer, and fry in batches, flipping each fritter once, until they are golden brown, about 2 minutes per side. Transfer the fried fritters to the oven to keep warm, and repeat until all the fritters have been fried.

6   Serve the warm fritters with the garlic buttermilk dip alongside.

SQUID WITH WATERMELON AND BASIL

serves 4 · TIME: 20 minutes preparation, 1 to 2 hours marination

Along the South Carolina coast, shrimpers land a variety of squid called "brief squid" as a bycatch that rarely hits the local market. Nevertheless, the fresh squid we find in our grocery stores is delicious—as scrumptious as shrimp, and slightly easier to prepare. It takes about the same time to cook (45 seconds in a pot of boiling water), but with squid, there are no shells to peel!

In this recipe, we marry squid with watermelon, a fruit that is so much more versatile than those summer picnics would suggest. We like to include diced melon in salads, where its crunch and moderate sweetness bring a welcome jolt of fun. It's especially delicious when paired with the acidity of lime or vinegar (as you already know if you've made yourself some Watermelon Margaritas, page 30, or Watermelon and Onion Pickles, page 71). The melons grown in the sandy soil on Johns Island outside Charleston have terrific flavor, and also a firm, snappy flesh that holds up well in the vinegar-chile-onion marinade here.

After the marination, we finish each serving with a drizzle of olive oil and a sprinkling of aromatic chopped fresh basil. It's a pretty dish to add to a summer buffet, with layers of color and flavor that epitomize *Simple Fresh Southern.*

---

1 tablespoon plus 2 teaspoons kosher salt, or more to taste

1 large lemon, halved

1 pound cleaned squid (see Squid Shopping Notes, page 90), cut into ⅓-inch-wide rings, flapper cut into strips, tentacle clusters cut in half

One 8-ounce piece seedless watermelon, cut into 1-x-1-x-¼-inch tiles (about 2 cups)

1 medium red onion, finely diced (about 1 cup)

1 jalapeño chile (optional), seeded and finely diced

¾ cup red wine vinegar

½ teaspoon freshly ground black pepper, or more to taste

¼ cup extra-virgin olive oil

Leaves from 3 sprigs fresh basil, coarsely chopped (about ¼ cup)

---

1   Combine 1 quart water and 1 tablespoon of the salt in a saucepan and bring to a boil. Juice the lemon into the water. Add the squid and cook for 45 seconds. With a slotted spoon or a skimmer, transfer the squid to an ice bath (or to a colander set under cold running water) to cool and halt the cooking. Reserve 2 cups of the squid cooking liquid. Drain the cooled squid and reserve it in a medium bowl.

2   Add ½ cup water, the watermelon pieces, onion, jalapeño, red wine vinegar, remaining 2 teaspoons salt, and the black pepper to the bowl and toss until evenly combined. If the level of the liquid is below the level of

(recipe continues)

the squid, add enough of the reserved squid cooking liquid to just cover. Pat a piece of plastic wrap directly on the surface of the liquid, and place the bowl in the refrigerator until the flavors have melded, 1 to 2 hours.

bed it down!
...

This squid dish makes an impressive luncheon salad when served over a bed of arugula or any leafy salad greens: Drain the squid of its marinating liquid and dress the salad greens, tossing them with the marinade and salt and pepper to taste. Divide the greens among the plates and spoon the squid and watermelon over them. Then drizzle the oil over the salad, and sprinkle with the basil.

3 To serve, use a slotted spoon to transfer serving portions of the squid and watermelon to small bowls. Drizzle each portion with a tablespoon of the olive oil and sprinkle about a tablespoon of the chopped basil over the top. Season each portion with salt, pepper, and marinating liquid to taste.

squid shopping notes
··· Most squid in fish markets comes with its beak and ink sac removed, but to be certain, ask your fishmonger for "cleaned" squid, and he or she can do that work for you, which saves some prep time. In your area, squid may only be available frozen, which is fine. Squid's unique rubbery texture holds up to freezing very well (and in fact, some cooks claim that freezing tenderizes the squid). Simply thaw frozen squid completely in a large bowl of cold water before you begin.

COCKTAIL EGGS WITH
PIMENTOS AND COUNTRY HAM

serves 4 · TIME: 20 minutes cooking, 5 minutes preparation

We set out these dressed-up hard-boiled eggs on plates at cocktail hour. They're so deceptively simple—a quarter egg and a slice of roasted pepper rolled up in thinly sliced country ham. People tend to giggle when they see them—*What? Southern breakfast on an hors d'oeuvre platter?*—but the twenty-four pieces this recipe makes tend to disappear before the twittering subsides. You could roast the pepper yourself—for instructions, see Roasted Red Pepper and Corn Salad with Tuna, page 135—but the spirit of this dish is way more laid-back than that. Pimentos from a jar are fine. And another thing: We use our hands to pick them up off the platter, but you could spear each egg with an upright toothpick for a swankier gathering.

6 large eggs	1 teaspoon white wine vinegar	4 ounces uncooked country ham, prosciutto, or Serrano ham (see Country Ham Shopping Notes, page 163)
4 ounces roasted red pepper (about 2 whole peppers)	¼ teaspoon coarsely ground black pepper	
1 tablespoon extra-virgin olive oil		

1 Fill a saucepan with a quart of water and bring to a boil. Turn the heat to low, and when the water simmers calmly, add the eggs gently, lowering them to the bottom two at a time with a large ladle. Let the eggs cook at a simmer exactly 14 minutes, drain them, and rinse under cold water until they're cool enough to handle, about 2 minutes. Peel the eggs and slice them in quarters lengthwise.

2 While the eggs cook, slice each roasted pepper into 12 strips about ⅓ inch wide. Place the peppers in a small bowl, add the olive oil, vinegar, and black pepper, and toss until evenly combined.

3 Cut the country ham into strips about 1 inch wide and 3 inches long. To assemble each cocktail egg, lay a strip of country ham flat on a cutting board, then lay an egg quarter and a strip of roasted pepper across one end of the strip and roll that end of the ham up and over the egg, continuing to roll it until it forms a small parcel. Place the eggs on a platter and serve.

BUTTERMILK FRESH CHEESE AND
11 DELICIOUS THINGS TO DO WITH IT

makes one 6-ounce round, enough for 4 as a snack, with crackers
TIME: 10 minutes cooking, 20 minutes cooling

I f you can boil water, you can make this buttermilk cheese—kin to Italian ricotta and Mexican queso fresco—which has become as much a part of our southern kitchen as cornbread or grits. It could not be easier to prepare: just heat a quart of milk with a cup and a half of buttermilk and any salt or dried seasonings, and when the curds have separated from the whey, pour the whole slosh through a fine-mesh strainer or cheesecloth to drain off the whey. Serve the cheese immediately, warm and soft, like ricotta, with a drizzle of olive oil, some sea salt, and freshly ground black pepper, or let it cool down and firm up a bit. That's all!

We think it's even more versatile than butter or cream cheese. You can spread it on cornbread and top it with a drizzle of honey or sorghum syrup. Make tomato sandwiches with it at the height of summer. Wrap little morsels up with country ham in collard-green wrappers to make deliciously creamy-salty hors d'oeuvre parcels. Crumble the cheese into all manner of salads and side dishes—see the garnish ideas in the Hot Sides chapter—to give them a mellow-flavored richness.

| 1 quart whole milk | 1½ cups whole or lowfat buttermilk | 2 teaspoons kosher salt |

1   Line a colander or a medium strainer with a triple layer of cheesecloth that's 12 inches square. Set the colander in the sink. (If you plan to preserve the whey for poaching liquid or Whey Sorbet, page 96, place the colander in a baking dish.)

2   Combine the milk, buttermilk, and salt in a large heavy-bottomed pot, and heat over medium-high heat until the mixture has separated into white curds and translucent whey, about 8 minutes. (If using lowfat buttermilk, separation occurs at about 180°F, and the curds will clump together readily; if using whole buttermilk, separation occurs closer to the boiling point, about 212°F, and the curds are finer-grained. When using

(recipe continues)

COUNTRY HAM AND FRESH CHEESE ROLLED
UP IN BLANCHED COLLARDS (PAGE 96)

whole buttermilk, let the pot of curds and whey stand off the heat for about 3 minutes after separation, so the curds cling tighter and facilitate the straining step.)

3   Ladle the contents of the pot into the cheesecloth-lined colander. Once the whey has drained (1 to 2 minutes), lift the corners of the cheesecloth and gather them together. Gently twist the gathered cloth over the cheese to press any excess whey out of it.

4   You can unwrap the cheese at this point and serve it immediately; or you can leave the cheese to drain further and cool to room temperature, about 10 minutes, before serving it. To serve a firmer cheese later, transfer the cheese, in its cloth, to a small flat-bottomed plate or pie pan and let stand in the refrigerator until cool, about 10 minutes. Then unwrap the cheese, gently invert it onto the plate, and discard the cloth. Tent the cheese with plastic wrap and keep it in the refrigerator until 10 minutes before you're ready to serve it, but not more than 2 days.

NOTE   The whey that's a by-product of making buttermilk fresh cheese is a perfectly seasoned, silky poaching liquid for cooking up some exceptionally tender and flavorful fish, chicken, or pork. Each cheese recipe yields about 4 cups of whey, which will keep, covered, in the refrigerator for about 2 days. It's just the right amount for poaching two chicken breasts or two ½-pound fish fillets in a medium sauté pan.

VARIATIONS

black pepper fresh cheese   To create a cheese with a prickle of heat and an alluring speckled appearance, add 1 teaspoon freshly ground black pepper to the milk-buttermilk mixture as it heats.

lemon zest fresh cheese   Add 1 teaspoon grated lemon zest to the milk-buttermilk mixture as it heats to create a cheese with an aromatic lemony flavor. Serve the cheese, still warm, on thinly sliced French bread, with a drizzle of extra-virgin olive oil and a pinch of salt.

herbed fresh cheese Add 1 teaspoon of your favorite dried herb— tarragon, oregano, and basil all work wonderfully—to the milk-buttermilk mixture as it heats, to create a cheese with a savory perfume.

vanilla fresh cheese Omit the salt and add 2 tablespoons of sugar and 1 teaspoon vanilla extract to the milk-buttermilk mixture as it heats to make a cheese for crumbling over Fruit Salad, page 235. The whey from this cheese makes a superb, beguiling Whey Sorbet, page 96.

buttermilk fresh cheese snack ideas

SIMPLEST

"smoked" fresh cheese Place the round of cheese on a plate and dust it with ¼ teaspoon smoked paprika, pinches of Maldon or kosher salt, and a grind of fresh black pepper. Surround it with crackers and watch it disappear.

pecan-crusted fresh cheese Toast ¼ cup pecan halves in a skillet until fragrant. Let them cool on a plate. Then "crust" the cheese by processing the pecans to fine crumbs and dredging the cheese in them. Alternatively, you can chop the nuts coarsely with a chef's knife, scatter them over and around the cheese, and drizzle honey over the plate—which makes a fantastic cheese- or dessert-course presentation, too.

fresh cheese garlanded with roasted red peppers, olive oil, and lemon Slice a few store-bought roasted red peppers or pimentos into thin slivers, and mound them over the top of the cheese. Drizzle with extra-virgin olive oil, squeeze half a lemon over it, and sprinkle with pinches of Maldon salt or kosher salt and a grind of black pepper. Serve with toasted slices of French bread or white toast points.

(recipe continues)

SIMPLE

basil fresh cheese wrapped in roasted red pepper strips
Make a round of Herbed Fresh Cheese with dried basil. Cut high-quality store-bought roasted red peppers or Spanish piquillo peppers into strips about ½ inch wide. Lay each pepper strip flat, place a rounded teaspoon of cheese at one end, roll it up, and seal with a toothpick. Place on a platter so they're easy to pick up.

tarragon fresh cheese and broiled grapes on french bread toasts Make a round of Herbed Fresh Cheese with dried tarragon. Toss 1½ cups seedless grapes with a tablespoon of olive oil, a tablespoon of your favorite vinegar, and some fresh herbs. Broil until the grapes are blackened and collapsing, about 10 minutes. Spread French bread toasts with some of the fresh cheese, and spoon the grapes and their juices over them.

country ham and fresh cheese rolled up in blanched collards Blanch 8 to 10 collard green leaves in 2 quarts boiling salty water (1 tablespoon kosher salt per quart) until tender, 6 to 8 minutes. Cut the rib out of each collard leaf so you're left with 2 halves. In each half leaf, roll up a sliver of country ham and a rounded teaspoon of the fresh cheese. You should end up with about 12 to 14 parcels per round of fresh cheese.

whey sorbet The whey produced from making Vanilla Fresh Cheese (page 94) makes a palate-cleansing dessert sorbet. Simply preserve the whey by straining the curds over a baking dish—you should have about a quart of whey. You can make whey sorbet from Buttermilk Fresh Cheese (page 93), but you'll need to reduce the salt in the original recipe to 1 teaspoon, and season the whey to taste with honey and lemon juice while it is still warm. Let the whey cool to room temperature, and transfer to the refrigerator. (Whey will keep, covered, in the refrigerator for 2 days.) Pour the whey into an ice cream maker and churn according to the manufacturer's instructions.

SMOKED SHRIMP WITH 3 DIPPING SAUCES

serves 8 as a snack or 4 as an appetizer • TIME: **30 minutes**

Smoking shrimp with a stovetop smoker creates a thrillingly addictive, fun-to-eat cocktail-hour food that's also a great appetizer.

"Wait! What?" you're saying. "A stovetop smoker?"

Yes, there is such a thing and if you don't own one (Athena, Camerons, and Nordic Ware are top brands), you can make one in a pinch, as long as you have a stainless steel or aluminum roasting pan and a flat roasting rack that fits inside it. The smoking chips you use in a stovetop smoker are like a coarse sawdust. They're made from a variety of hardwoods—apple, cherry, and hickory are most common—and you can buy them at department stores such as Target and Wal-Mart, or from cookware retailers like Williams-Sonoma. Learning your way around a stovetop smoker (see Notes on Successful Stovetop Smoking, page 98) adds a new vector of creative exploration to your repertoire (see Smoked Cauliflower, page 166, and Smoked Trout, page 198).

Serve these smoked shrimp with one or all three dipping sauces.

1 pound headless large shell-on shrimp (26 to 30 per pound; see Notes on Deveining Shrimp, page 61, and Shrimp Shopping Notes, page 63)	**LEMON CHIVE MAYO** ½ cup high-quality store-bought mayonnaise, such as Hellmann's or Duke's	**SRIRACHA BUTTERMILK DIP** ¼ cup buttermilk ¼ cup sour cream
½ recipe Garlic Buttermilk Dip (page 86)	¼ cup sour cream 2 tablespoons chopped fresh chives ¼ teaspoon grated lemon zest 2 tablespoons fresh lemon juice ½ teaspoon kosher salt, plus more to taste	2 teaspoons Thai chili sauce (sriracha), plus more to taste

Put 1 tablespoon applewood chips in the center of your stovetop smoker pan, or in the center of a 9-x-13-inch stainless steel or aluminum roasting pan. Lay the shrimp on their sides on the rack of your smoker. (If using a conventional roasting pan and rack, wrap the roasting rack in aluminum foil, then place it in the pan, and lay the shrimp on their sides in a even layer on the rack.) Cover the smoker only partly; if using a roasting pan, cover with aluminum foil, crimping the edges tightly but leaving one corner uncrimped. Turn the burner to medium and center the pan above it.

(recipe continues)

When you see the first wisp of smoke rise from the smoker or pan, cover it completely and continue to smoke until the shrimp are pale orange, firm, and cooked through, 20 to 25 minutes.

2   While the shrimp are smoking, prepare any or all of the dipping sauces by whisking the ingredients together in a separate bowl.

3   When the shrimp are done, you can either serve them immediately, smoker-warm, or let them cool to room temperature and then refrigerate them until ready to serve, but not for more than 2 days. Either way, serve the dipping sauces alongside.

notes on successful stovetop smoking …

- On discoloration of the smoker pan: Using a brand-new stainless steel stovetop smoker (like the ones Camerons Cookware and Max Burton by Athena make) for the first time is bittersweet because its shiny pristine surface discolors to an oily brown, but that is to be expected. If you're using a roasting pan as a stovetop smoker, be aware that it will discolor as well, so if you prefer your roasting pan looking nice and shiny, you may simply want to buy a stovetop smoker or a second inexpensive roasting pan to devote exclusively to smoking.

- On vigilance with respect to stovetop smoking: Because stovetop smoking calls for the application of direct heat to a dry pan, vigilance is required. Why? Because you'll have no aural cues—the sizzling of a skillet of onions, say—to remind you that the pan is very, very hot.

SOUPS

Liquid nourishment is often overlooked in the headlong rush to put food, solid food, on the table, but soups can be one of the most effective ways to deliver flavor and refreshment. Most soups are easy to prepare ahead, in quantity, and they make terrific leftovers, since they reheat easily and often improve with a little time in the fridge. If, like us, you enjoy experimenting in your kitchen, then you'll appreciate how soups take on impromptu seasonings and ingredients—look at what I found at the back of the spice cabinet!—in a flash.

Soups don't have to fit into the Campbell's range of options, either. Lique-fying your favorite ingredients, even ones you don't expect to find in a soup, like bread to thicken a tomato bisque or lettuce (see our Lettuce Soup, page 107), can produce some great results.

We have endeavored to give all the soups here delicious flavor but also a riveting structure: like the spine of acidity in the Chilled Tomato Soup, page 112, or the textural contrast in the Creamy Asparagus Soup with Grilled Asparagus, page 115, or the satisfying inversion of the Oyster Soup, page 103, where the oysters enter each serving bowl first, followed by ladles of hot bisque, which gently cooks them to perfection.

OYSTER SOUP (PAGE 103)

RECIPES

Oyster Soup

Fresh Vegetable Broth

Collard Greens and Winter Roots Soup

Creamy Sweet-Onion Soup

Lettuce Soup

Butternut Squash Soup with Rosemary

White Gazpacho

Chilled Tomato Soup

Creamy Asparagus Soup
with Grilled Asparagus

Hominy Stew with Chicken and Chiles

OYSTER SOUP

serves 2 to 4 • TIME: 15 minutes

Oyster stews thick enough to hold a spoon straight up are missing the point: it's about the oysters, not the cream (and cornstarch or flour or whatever else they use to accomplish this unappetizing feat). Our light bisque uses cream only judiciously—and a splash of white wine and a wisp of nutmeg—so that the briny flavor of the oysters is front and center. Serve it with a side dish of Collard Greens with Poblano Chiles and Chorizo (page 146), and a glass of the white wine you used in the soup, for a perfect supper.

3 tablespoons unsalted butter	¼ teaspoon crushed dried red chile flakes	1 pint freshly shucked oysters with their liquor (about 24 pieces), oysters and liquor reserved separately (see Oyster Shopping Notes, page 79)
1 bunch scallions (6 to 8 scallions), white and green parts thinly sliced and kept separate	½ cup Bar Harbor or Look's Atlantic brand clam juice	
	½ cup dry white wine, such as Sauvignon Blanc or unoaked Chardonnay	
1 teaspoon kosher salt, plus more to taste		2 cups whole milk
⅛ teaspoon freshly grated nutmeg		½ cup heavy cream

1   In a 3-quart saucepan or stockpot, melt the butter over medium heat until frothy. Add the sliced white parts of the scallions and the salt, nutmeg, and chile flakes. Sauté, stirring, until the scallions are fragrant and translucent, 2 to 3 minutes. Add the clam juice, wine, and oyster liquor, and continue to cook until the liquid is reduced by half, about 6 minutes. Add the milk and the cream and cook until the soup just steams, to avoid separation.

2   Divide the oysters among 4 warm bowls. Remove the hot soup from the stove and ladle it directly over the raw oysters in their bowls. Shower with the scallion greens and serve.

garnish it smoky
• • •
Smoke-cured ham is a superb garnish for this soup. Sprinkle some diced-up golden-browned slab bacon or paper-thin shavings of uncooked country ham or prosciutto on the surface of the soup just before serving.

FRESH VEGETABLE BROTH

makes 1 quart • TIME: 10 minutes

When there are decent brands of vegetable broth on the market, making your own would seem as crazy as blowing your own lightbulbs or fashioning paper clips out of a spool of wire. Do us a favor and try it just once. You'll be blown away by the bright, fresh vegetable flavor this raw juice adds when you start a soup, risotto, or grits with it. Our no-cook recipe isn't complicated: to a bunch of fresh celery, we add 2 pounds watery vegetables such as tomatoes, green peppers, cucumbers, radishes, turnips, or tomatillos—whatever you happen to have on hand—plus any small amounts of other nonwatery vegetables such as potatoes, carrots, and winter squash, or crisp herbs like dill and parsley that are still alive in your fridge (we avoid dry, fibrous veggies like eggplant or summer squash). You buzz them all up in a food processor with 2 cups of water and strain it, and the resulting juice has a natural sweetness and intensity that will make the store-bought version seem insipid. We use this broth to make our best-tasting grits ever—it's as if the corn grits are thanking us for dignifying them with such a special liquid!

| 1 bunch celery, sliced | 2 pounds watery vegetables (see headnote), trimmed and coarsely chopped | 1 teaspoon kosher salt |

Combine the celery, vegetables, salt, and 2 cups water in a food processor (or, in batches, in a blender) and liquefy. Strain through a fine-mesh strainer and store in a sealed container in the refrigerator for no more than 1 week. This broth freezes brilliantly, but may take on freezer odors after more than 2 weeks.

COLLARD GREENS AND WINTER ROOTS SOUP

serves 4 • TIME: 10 minutes preparation, 40 minutes cooking

Any dishwasher who has ever faced the soupy ends of a well-seasoned pot of collards on January 2nd knows that the cooking broth is positively energizing to drink, packed with vitamins and a deep, rootsy flavor that gives you goose bumps, it's so good. So we've taken to serving shot glasses of it to bleary-eyed houseguests for brunch, poaching eggs in it, and finally acknowledging that collards alone would make a terrific soup. We developed our collards soup—a stew, really—to mimic the incomparable long-stewed-greens flavor of that collards pot, but added some roots (turnips and carrots) to sweeten it and beans to give the dish more protein and rib-sticking potential.

---

1 tablespoon extra-virgin olive oil

3 ounces slab bacon, or 3 strips thick-cut bacon, diced

1 medium yellow onion, chopped (about 1 cup)

1 large yellow turnip, peeled and diced (about 2 cups)

2 small carrots, peeled, halved lengthwise, and cut into ½-inch-thick half-moons

4 cloves garlic, minced

1½ pounds collard greens (about 1 bunch), ribs removed, leaves finely chopped (about 1 packed quart)

2 tablespoons white wine vinegar

½ teaspoon kosher salt, plus more to taste

¼ teaspoon crushed dried red chile flakes

¼ teaspoon freshly ground black pepper, plus more to taste

1 quart vegetable broth, homemade (page 104) or store-bought

One 14-ounce can white cannellini or navy beans, drained

---

1   Pour the oil into a 4- to 6-quart Dutch oven or stockpot set over medium-high heat. When the oil shimmers, add the bacon and sauté until it has rendered some of its fat, about 3 minutes. Add the onion, turnip, carrots, and garlic, and cook, stirring, until the onions are softened and translucent, about 3 minutes. Add the collards a handful at a time, turning them until they wilt before adding more.

2   When all the collards have wilted (about 4 minutes), add the vinegar, salt, chile flakes, and black pepper. Add the vegetable broth, beans, and 2 cups water, and cover the pot. When the soup comes to a boil, turn the heat to low. Simmer until the carrots and turnips are tender, about 30 minutes.

3   Season the soup to taste with salt and black pepper. Serve immediately or let cool to room temperature, cover, and store in the refrigerator for up to 3 days.

CREAMY SWEET-ONION SOUP

serves 4 • TIME: 10 minutes preparation, about 1 hour cooking

We make this decadently creamy onion soup with the sweet Vidalia onions that are grown in southeast Georgia and harvested from May until October. And while this recipe, which takes more than an hour to prepare, would seem to challenge at least one of the three principles of *Simple Fresh Southern,* the method here is so easy, the number of ingredients so few and so readily available, and the flavor so blissfully divine that we simply—no pun intended—had to include it.

1 cup (2 sticks) unsalted butter	1 teaspoon kosher salt, plus more to taste	2 cups dry white wine, such as Pinot Grigio
¼ cup extra-virgin olive oil	½ teaspoon freshly ground black pepper, plus more to taste	1 pint heavy cream
3 pounds sweet onions, such as Vidalia, halved lengthwise and thinly sliced		1 small bunch fresh chives, thinly sliced (¼ cup)

1 In a 4-quart Dutch oven or heavy-bottomed stockpot, melt the butter with the olive oil over medium-high heat until frothy. Add the onions, salt, and black pepper, and sauté, stirring frequently and taking care not to let the onions brown, for 10 minutes. Turn heat to low, cover, and continue to cook until they are completely soft and tender, about 20 minutes.

2 Add the wine and cream and simmer, uncovered, until reduced by half, about 30 minutes.

3 Transfer the soup, in batches, to a food processor or blender, and puree until smooth. Pour the soup back into the stockpot and return it to serving temperature (if necessary) over low heat. Season to taste with salt and black pepper, and serve immediately in bowls, garnished with a sprinkle of chives. (Covered, the soup will keep in the refrigerator for about 3 days.)

LETTUCE SOUP

Those poor tender lettuces that farmers coddle and pamper and carefully deliver to market are often smothered to death on the plate by cheesy or bossy salad dressings. Every now and then we have to remind ourselves what lettuce really tastes like. This easy recipe distills and concentrates the leaves' fresh, light essence into a soup. The slight tang of buttermilk complements and we think amplifies the green flavors beautifully without upstaging the delicate star of the show. On an early summer day, cool lettuce soup served with a side dish of smoked shrimp is a perfect lunch.

2 cups vegetable broth, homemade (page 104) or store-bought, chilled	1 head green leaf lettuce (about 12 ounces), rinsed well and cut into fine shreds	2 teaspoons kosher salt, plus more to taste
1 cup whole or lowfat buttermilk, chilled	8 ounces romaine lettuce hearts, rinsed well and cut into fine shreds	Freshly ground black pepper to taste
3 cloves garlic, chopped		

Pour the vegetable broth and buttermilk into a blender. Add the garlic, half the shredded lettuces, and the salt. Liquefy on the blender's highest setting for 1 minute. Add the remaining lettuce and repeat. Season to taste with salt and black pepper. (Covered, the soup will keep in the refrigerator for about 3 days.)

BUTTERNUT SQUASH SOUP WITH ROSEMARY

serves 4 to 6 • TIME: 30 minutes

n preparing the family Thanksgiving meal, one of us usually tackles the "Thanksgiving Baroque"—the heirloom American Bronze turkey, brined, rubbed with paprika butter, then stuffed with oysters and chestnuts (a three-day production)—while the other brother heads for the relative ease of the "Thanksgiving Zen," or those simple dishes that express clear flavors with a minimum of effort and agita. Inevitably it's the Zen dishes, the meditations on one or two ingredients, that get the wildest raves. The noble butternut, the most utilitarian (and fortunately the tastiest) supermarket squash, breaks down into a silky soup, which we highlight with wintery, medieval rosemary and cured ham. A little garlic and buttermilk serve to amp up the flavor of the butternut. It's a rich enough dish to make a fine lunch, served with a thick wedge of buttered toasted bread and a glass of dry French Chardonnay (or any elegant white wine that's not too fruity).

I tablespoon extra-virgin olive oil

I teaspoon minced fresh rosemary

⅓ cup finely diced country ham or Serrano ham (about 1¼ ounces)

I tablespoon minced garlic (about 3 large cloves)

One 2-pound butternut squash, peeled, seeded, and cut into ½-inch dice (4 cups)

1½ teaspoons kosher salt, or to taste

¼ cup whole or lowfat buttermilk, plus more for garnish

Freshly ground black pepper, for garnish

1 Pour the olive oil into a 12-inch skillet set over medium-low heat. Once the oil warms, add the rosemary, ham, and garlic and stir constantly for about 2 minutes, until the garlic is fragrant but not browning.

2 Turn the heat to low, add the squash, and stir for about 30 seconds to coat the pieces with the oil. Let cook for a minute longer, still stirring. Then add 3 cups water and cover the skillet. Turn up the heat to medium-high and bring to a boil. Turn down the heat so that the liquid is simmering, stir in the salt, and cook, covered, for 7 minutes, until the squash is tender but not dissolving into the soup.

3 Using an immersion blender or transferring the mixture to a food processor (in batches if necessary), blend the soup until just a few chunks of squash and ham are still visible in the puree. Add the buttermilk and stir to incorporate. Serve in large bowls, and as a final touch, loosely stir a tablespoon of buttermilk into each, leaving a trail of white. Season with a grind of black pepper.

WHITE GAZPACHO

serves 6 • TIME: 20 minutes preparation, 30 minutes refrigeration

Nothing breaks the heat of a South Carolina summer like a cool, pale green "white" gazpacho served in a ceramic bowl beaded with condensation. Cucumbers are the main ingredient, enriched with yogurt and spiced with a little fresh garlic and jalapeño. We love to jazz up the colors of the soup—and give it a dash of sweetness—with a garnish of red tomato salsa.

3 medium tomatoes (about 1 pound)

1 small yellow onion, finely diced (½ cup)

2 heaping tablespoons finely chopped fresh cilantro (about 6 sprigs)

2 tablespoons distilled white vinegar, white wine vinegar, or champagne vinegar

Kosher salt to taste

Freshly ground black pepper to taste

4 medium cucumbers, peeled, seeded, and cut into large dice (about 3 cups)

2 small jalapeño chiles, seeded and finely diced (about 2 tablespoons)

2 cloves garlic, minced

1 cup vegetable broth, homemade (page 104) or store-bought

2 cups plain yogurt

1 Set a strainer over a medium bowl. Core the tomatoes, cut them in half crosswise, and using your pinkie finger, tease the seeds out of the cavities, letting them drop into the strainer. Tap the rim of the strainer against your palm for 30 seconds, until most of the flavorful gel clinging to the seeds dissolves and drips into the bowl. Discard the seeds.

2 Finely dice the tomatoes and transfer them to the bowl with the tomato water. Add the onion, cilantro, and vinegar, and toss. Season the salsa to taste with salt and black pepper, and refrigerate it. (Salsa will keep 3 days in the refrigerator.) Place the soup bowls you intend to use in the refrigerator, too.

3 Combine the cucumbers, chiles, garlic, vegetable broth, and yogurt in a food processor, and pulse until smooth. Season to taste with salt and black pepper, and chill for at least 30 minutes and up to 3 days.

4 Divide the soup among the chilled bowls, and garnish each serving with a couple spoonfuls of the salsa.

CHILLED TOMATO SOUP

serves 4 • TIME: 20 minutes

There's really no fruit or vegetable that compares to a tomato ripened on the vine, is there? Its freshness, assertiveness, and multidimensional fruity/acidic/sweet profile has more in common with a glass of wine than with a cucumber or a kiwi. We like to put the tomato's unique personality front and center with this super-minimal, super-simple tomato soup; just a little bit of red wine vinegar, some lightly softened onion, and a few pinches of smoked paprika ensure that it's dinner rather than dessert. A burstingly ripe heirloom variety of tomato, like a Yoder's German Yellow, would be ideal for this recipe, but any vine-ripened tomato (most grocery stores carry them these days, a few vivid fruits clinging to a snippet of vine) will work perfectly. Serve the soup with hot buttered toast cut into points.

2 pounds vine-ripened tomatoes (about 6 tomatoes)	⅛ teaspoon smoked sweet paprika	Chopped fresh herbs, for garnish (whatever is available, such as chives, lovage, celery tops, or basil)
2 tablespoons extra-virgin olive oil, plus more for garnish	2 tablespoons red wine vinegar	
	½ cup whole or lowfat buttermilk (optional; omit for a vegan-friendly recipe)	Best-quality extra-virgin olive oil, for garnish (see Notes on Finishing, page 159)
1 medium onion, chopped (about 1 cup)		
1½ teaspoons kosher salt		

1. Set a strainer over a bowl. Core the tomatoes, cut them in half crosswise, and using your pinkie finger, tease the seeds out of the cavities, letting them drop into the strainer. Tap the rim of the strainer against your palm for 30 seconds, until most of the flavorful gel clinging to the seeds dissolves and drips into the bowl. Discard the seeds. Put the tomatoes in a food processor and add the tomato water.

2. Heat the oil in a medium sauté pan or skillet over medium-high heat. Add the onion, ½ teaspoon of the salt, and the smoked paprika, and sauté until the onions are translucent and very fragrant, about 4 minutes. Transfer the contents of the sauté pan to the processor, adding them to the tomatoes and juice. Add the vinegar and the remaining salt, and process until the contents liquefy.

3. Add the buttermilk, if desired, and whisk thoroughly to incorporate it. Serve the soup chilled, garnished with a few pinches of herbs and a drizzle of your best olive oil. (Covered, the soup will keep in the refrigerator for about 3 days.)

CREAMY ASPARAGUS SOUP WITH GRILLED ASPARAGUS

serves 4 as a luncheon main course or 8 as a first course • TIME: 20 minutes

This soup is best in the spring, when local asparagus is in season in North America and when you're most likely to be anticipating the grilling season. Here we coax the maximum fresh green flavor out of the asparagus stems, then char the tender asparagus tops in a skillet until they've got that grilled-asparagus deliciousness. We float the tops on the surface of the soup to create a dish that's super-easy, and yet has layers and layers of flavor.

3 pounds asparagus (about 2 large bunches)	I medium yellow onion, coarsely chopped (about I cup)	I to 2 ounces thinly sliced country ham or prosciutto Americano, cut into strips
I quart vegetable broth, homemade (page 104) or store-bought	2 teaspoons grapeseed, canola, or other vegetable oil	Freshly ground black pepper to taste
¾ teaspoon kosher salt	½ cup heavy cream or whole or lowfat buttermilk, or to taste	

1 Trim any woody parts from the stem ends of the asparagus. Cut the tops from the asparagus about 2 inches down from the tip, and reserve. Cut the spears crosswise into pieces about ¾ inch long.

2 Bring the vegetable broth and ¼ teaspoon of the salt to a simmer in a 4- to 6-quart pot, and add the chopped asparagus spears and onion. Add all but 24 of the asparagus tops to the pot, too. Simmer until the asparagus spears are tender, 10 to 12 minutes.

3 While the broth and the veggies simmer, pour the oil into a cast-iron skillet or sauté pan and heat it over high heat, tilting the pan occasionally so the oil coats the bottom thinly and evenly. When the oil begins to smoke, add the reserved asparagus tops, and scatter the remaining ½ teaspoon salt over them. Cook, stirring only every 1 to 1½ minutes, until the asparagus tops are browned in places, about 6 minutes. Remove them from the heat.

4 Transfer the broth and vegetables to a blender (in batches, if necessary), and liquefy. Return the soup to the pot, add the heavy cream, and heat to a simmer. Serve immediately in bowls, garnished with the skillet-grilled asparagus tops, strips of country ham, and freshly ground black pepper. (Covered, the soup will keep in the refrigerator for about 3 days.)

HOMINY STEW WITH CHICKEN AND CHILES

serves 6 • TIME: **50 minutes**

The wonderfully nutty and hearty corn flavor of hominy (the rustic lime-treated corn kernels that are a keystone ingredient in many southern cuisines) combines beautifully with the flavor of sun-dried peppers and chicken in this stew, a close cousin of tortilla soup. The aroma rising from the pot is a reward all in itself with this dish, which we prepare when the temperature drops and we get a craving for something spicy, nourishing, and warm. And if we happen to get snowed in, chances are we have the ingredients in the cupboard or the fridge: canned hominy, dried chiles, chicken broth, a tomato, leftover chicken. Even the limes and cilantro in the garnish (you could substitute parsley) are standard ingredients in the crisper drawer of our fridge or at the corner store.

Though other varieties (mulato, ancho, guajillo) will do, pasilla chiles are worth seeking out for their raisiny, earthy flavor and mild heat. Rinsing the extra starch off canned hominy is an important step: doing so washes away any tinny taste and makes the corn flavor pop out, fresher and brighter than before.

Serve the stew with Mexican beer, dosed with a squirt of lime, or with a ripe Argentine chardonnay or New York State riesling.

- 1 tablespoon olive or canola oil
- 1 ounce dried pasilla chiles (2 to 4 large chiles), stemmed and seeded
- 1 large red onion, halved and sliced into thin half-moons (about 1¾ cups)
- 1 medium tomato, seeded and coarsely chopped (¾ cup)

- One 36.5-ounce can white hominy, drained and rinsed
- Two 14.5-ounce cans (3 generous cups) chicken broth
- ½ teaspoon kosher salt, plus more to taste
- 2 cups shredded cooked chicken

- 1 cup dry white wine
- 1 small bunch cilantro, chopped (about ½ cup)
- 3 scallions (white and green parts), cut into thin disks
- 2 limes, quartered

---

1 Pour the olive oil into a 3-quart pot and set it over medium-high heat. When the oil shimmers, add the chiles and cook, flattening them occasionally with a spatula, until they begin to turn fragrant, about 30 seconds per side, and reserve. Add the onion and tomato and cook, stirring every minute or so, until the onions begin to brown at the edges and the mixture smells sweet, about 5 minutes.

2 Add the hominy, chicken broth, and toasted chiles. Cover, and when the brew begins to simmer, turn the heat down to low. Simmer for 10 minutes, by which time you should smell the fragrance of corn and chiles in equal measure emanating from the pot.

3 Add the salt and puree the mixture, in batches if necessary, in a blender or food processor.

4 While the puree is in the blender, add the chicken and the wine to the empty pot, and bring to a simmer over medium heat. When the wine has simmered for 2 full minutes and the chicken is beginning to soften, return the puree to the pot and stir to incorporate. Season with salt if necessary, return to a simmer, and you're done. Stir once before serving. Garnish each bowl with a couple generous pinches of chopped cilantro, plenty of sliced scallions, and a lime quarter, squeezed into the bowl. (Covered, the stew will keep in the refrigerator for about 3 days.)

salads and cold sides

We believe even routine weeknight meals can be symphonic, with complementary layers of flavor, texture, and color, as well as thrilling changes of tempo and mood. The main course on the plate—say, the Pork Tenderloins with Madeira and Fig Gravy, page 207, or Mushroom and Okra Purloo, page 186—might be the largo passage, whose comforting, languorous proteins lull you into savory bliss, while the salads and cold side dishes—cool, crisp slaws and leafy, green lettuces slicked with citrusy dressings—are the allegro: zesty, uptempo, pulse-quickening forkfuls that reawaken your palate.

In this chapter, we've collected our favorite salads and cold side dishes. All are easy to make and easy to eat, but they're designed to draw maximum flavor and potential from the ingredients. For example, in our Cucumber, Tomato, and Okra Salad (page 124), we toast sliced okra in a skillet, which brings out a warm, caramelized flavor, then scatter the pieces like croutons over a cucumber and tomato salad. And you'll find segmented citrus—whole lime sections—tossed into our Cabbage and Lime Salad with Roasted Peanuts (page 129): we think the lime is the perfect tonic to the spice and crunch of the cabbages.

We close the chapter with a cooled-down riff on the warm gingered beets we typically encounter in the South served as a side dish. Our Field Pea Salad with Gingered Beets and Lemon, page 139, is a hearty salad whose earthiness is brightened up with the zing of lemon and ginger. That's music to our ears!

CHERRY TOMATO AND SOYBEAN SALAD (PAGE 121)

RECIPES

Cherry Tomato and Soybean Salad

Easy Ambrosia

Cucumber, Tomato, and Okra Salad

Green Goddess Potato Salad

Cabbage and Lime Salad
with Roasted Peanuts

Carrot and Turnip Slaw with Dill

Snow Pea and Carrot Salad
with Ginger Dressing

Roasted Red Pepper and Corn Salad
with Tuna

Curried New Potato Salad

Field Pea Salad with Gingered Beets
and Lemon

Red Rice Salad

CHERRY TOMATO AND SOYBEAN SALAD

serves 4 · TIME: 15 minutes

Although soybeans have been grown in the Southeast since the 1820s, they only appeared in farmers markets in South Carolina about five years ago—the crop was more valuable in Asia. Fresh soybeans taste uncommonly nutty, and are a dynamite substitute for any butterbean or shell pea you might blanch, cool, and add to a summery salad. We should pause here to thank Japanese restaurants in North America, many of which serve soybeans in the shell, steamed and salted, as *edamame,* for popularizing soybean consumption in the United States. Now we can buy frozen shelled soybeans in supermarkets, so we make this summery salad year-round.

In this salad—one of our easiest and most beloved—we marry soybeans with the concentrated sweetness of cherry tomatoes. During the high tomato season, we use any one of a number of varieties of cherry tomatoes that grow in our garden beds. But the grape tomato that's available on supermarket shelves year-round nowadays is delicious in this recipe; these elongated cherry tomatoes came to market prominence recently and replaced, virtually overnight, the more rounded cherry tomato varieties. The former have a bold, impressive flavor that survives trucking across long distances. We applaud their presence in even the most anemic American supermarkets.

2½ teaspoons kosher salt, plus more to taste

1 pound fresh or frozen shelled soybeans (about 3¼ cups)

¾ cup whole or lowfat buttermilk

1 clove garlic, finely grated

2 tablespoons extra-virgin olive oil

10 ounces cherry or grape tomatoes (about 2 cups), halved lengthwise

Leaves from 4 sprigs fresh basil (about 1 cup loosely packed)

Freshly ground black pepper

---

1 Bring a quart of water to a boil in a large saucepan, and add 2 teaspoons of the salt. Add the soybeans and when the water returns to a boil, continue to cook until the soybeans are just tender but cooked through, about 5 minutes. Drain the beans in a colander and cool them under cold running water. Shake the colander vigorously to remove excess water.

2 In a medium bowl, whisk the remaining ½ teaspoon salt with the buttermilk, garlic, and olive oil. In a large bowl, toss the beans, tomatoes, and basil together. Pour the dressing over the salad, and toss to coat evenly. Season to taste with salt and freshly ground black pepper. (Covered, the salad will keep in the refrigerator for about 3 days.)

EASY AMBROSIA

serves 6 • **TIME: 5 minutes toasting, 10 minutes preparation**

*A*mbrosia, as it relates to food, means different things to different people. We discovered this when we traveled the country, teaching the recipes from our last book. (Our own ambrosia recipe is a savory salad of citrus, avocado, and coconut with a buttermilk-garlic-herb dressing; the ambrosia we ate as kids was a sweet-sour horror of mini marshmallows, canned pineapple, canned mandarin oranges, and mayo.)

We learned in our classes that many southerners grew up with another type of ambrosia, one that couldn't be simpler: fresh orange sections sprinkled with fresh (and sometimes toasted) coconut shavings. Very cool.

But we're attached to the idea of ambrosia as a savory, slightly bittersweet salad. Here, we've spun it into a parsley salad—parsley being something we can never get enough of. The flat-leaf (or Italian) parsley variety is essential here. If you can't find it, substitute a similar amount of chopped arugula or chopped fresh spinach.

Easy Ambrosia has become our go-to salad whenever we want to bring some zest to a humdrum weeknight.

---

1 tablespoon coconut flakes, preferably unsweetened

2 navel oranges or tangelos, segmented (see Segmenting Citrus, page 130)

1 ruby grapefruit, segmented

¾ teaspoon kosher salt

2 tablespoons extra-virgin olive oil

2 medium Belgian endive, root ends trimmed, cut lengthwise into thin strips

2 cups fresh flat-leaf parsley (from about one 3-ounce bunch), stems trimmed

---

1 Spread the coconut flakes in the broiler pan of a toaster oven and toast on a medium setting until they become ever so gently browned, about 5 minutes. (Alternatively, you could toast the coconut by stirring it in a dry skillet until it toasts and becomes fragrant.) Reserve.

2 Segment the oranges and the grapefruit over a large salad bowl to catch all the juice and segments. Drain the juice into a small bowl and add the salt and olive oil. Add the endive and parsley to the salad bowl with the citrus segments.

3 Whisk the citrus juice with the olive oil and salt until the dressing is emulsified. Pour the dressing over the salad, and toss until the salad is evenly coated. (Covered, the ambrosia will keep in the refrigerator for 1 day.) Before serving, sprinkle the reserved toasted coconut over it.

CUCUMBER, TOMATO, AND OKRA SALAD

serves 4 · TIME: 10 minutes preparation, 10 minutes cooking

Cook okra for a few minutes in a hot dry skillet and you get something very special and very delicious. "Skillet-toasted" okra is an easy treatment of our favorite vegetable that will make okra lovers out of skeptics. In the course of writing our first book, we decided we wanted to cook out the "rope"—the sliminess—in okra because we didn't want that texture in our Corn and Okra Pudding, and we loved the sweet caramelized-okra flavor that resulted. In this recipe, we treat the toasted okra almost as you would a crouton, scattering a portion over each serving of the salad.

Once you've skillet-toasted the okra, the rest of this salad can be thrown together easily, and all the ingredients can be found in the most pedestrian of supermarkets. Substitute plum or Roma tomatoes, pound for pound, if you can't get vine-ripened. You can use frozen okra, but be aware that its increased moisture content and its cooler temperature will double the time it takes to brown in the skillet.

We serve this salad often, in small serving bowls or as a cold side with a main dish, but you could serve it on a plate over a small bed of arugula or watercress.

---

8 ounces fresh okra, trimmed and cut crosswise into ½-inch-thick rounds (about 2 cups)

¾ teaspoon kosher salt, plus more to taste

1 pound vine-ripened tomatoes (about 3 tomatoes)

1 tablespoon Dijon mustard

1 tablespoon plus 1 teaspoon red wine vinegar

¼ cup extra-virgin olive oil

1 large seedless cucumber (1 pound), peeled, trimmed, and cut into large matchsticks (see Cucumber Shopping Notes, below)

3 tablespoons finely chopped scallions (white and green parts)

½ teaspoon freshly ground black pepper, plus more to taste

---

cucumber shopping notes ··· We call for seedless ("English") cucumbers here because they tend to have more flesh per pound than the standard ones with seeds. But even a cucumber labeled "seedless" may have at its core a membrane of flesh that carries little flavor and has a strange texture, so make sure you trim it from the cucumber. In this recipe, we trim the very ends of the cucumber, peel it, then slice it in half lengthwise. Then we trim the empty seed cavity with a melon baller or a small spoon. We slice each long half into three pieces, 2 to 2½ inches long, before proceeding to make large matchsticks.

1   Scatter the okra in a single layer in a dry 12-inch skillet
    or large sauté pan. Cook over medium-high heat, moving
    the pieces around frequently, until the okra is just
    browning around the edges, about 8 minutes. Remove
    from the heat, transfer the okra to a small bowl, and
    sprinkle ¼ teaspoon of the salt over it. Reserve.

2   Set a strainer over a medium bowl. Core the tomatoes,
    cut them in half widthwise, and using your pinkie finger,
    tease the seeds out of the cavities, letting them drop into
    the strainer. Tap the rim of the strainer against your
    palm for 30 seconds, until most of the flavorful gel
    clinging to the seeds dissolves and drips into the bowl.
    Discard the seeds. Chop the tomatoes.

3   Add the mustard, vinegar, and remaining ½ teaspoon
    salt to the tomato water, and whisk until the mustard is
    completely incorporated into the liquid. Add the olive oil in a thin stream,
    whisking constantly until the ingredients are thoroughly emulsified in a
    dressing of uniform, thick consistency.

4   In a large bowl, toss the cucumber with the tomatoes, scallions, and black
    pepper until thoroughly combined. Pour the dressing over the vegetables
    and toss until they're evenly coated. Season to taste with additional salt
    and black pepper, if needed.

5   Divide the salad evenly among 4 bowls, and sprinkle a handful of the
    salted toasted okra over each portion.

garnish it smoky
• • •
*With high-quality slab
bacon. After the okra has
finished toasting in the
skillet and been transferred
to the small bowl, scatter
2 ounces diced slab bacon
(or 2 slices thick-cut bacon,
diced) in the skillet, and
cook over medium-high heat
until it is firm and barely
browned, 3 to 4 minutes.
Drain on a plate lined with
a paper towel, and garnish
each finished salad plate
with the bacon.*

GREEN GODDESS POTATO SALAD

serves 4 • TIME: 25 minutes preparation, 15 minutes resting

Like red velvet cake, green goddess dressing is a recipe that was dreamed up in a fancy hotel kitchen far from the South, but appears so frequently in southern cookbooks published in the mid-twentieth century that we've adopted it as our own. And really, what southerner wouldn't? The name alone conjures images of herby, summer-garden bliss.

Green goddess is a mayonnaise-and-sour-cream dressing colored green with as many herbs as you'd like to add, and spiked with lemon juice and vinegar. The original recipe, invented in the kitchen of San Francisco's Palace Hotel in the 1920s, calls for scallions and parsley (though the current chef there, Jesse Llapitan, favors chervil and tarragon). Ours adds a powerful dose of fresh tarragon, and we're not shy with our black pepper either. Green goddess dressing is brilliant on everything from fried oysters to raw endive leaves. Here we adapt our recipe to a warm potato salad that's a hero side dish to almost any protein.

Unlike red velvet cake, green goddess dressing recipes never call for food coloring!

2 tablespoons plus 1 teaspoon kosher salt, plus more to taste	½ cup sour cream	2 anchovy fillets, minced, or ½ teaspoon anchovy paste (optional)
2½ pounds small red potatoes, peeled and cut into quarters	½ cup finely chopped scallions (white and green parts)	1 tablespoon white wine vinegar or champagne vinegar
½ cup high-quality store-bought mayonnaise, such as Hellmann's or Duke's	½ cup finely chopped fresh flat-leaf parsley	1 tablespoon fresh lime juice
	2 tablespoons finely chopped fresh tarragon	½ teaspoon freshly ground black pepper, plus more to taste

1   Fill a 4-quart stockpot half full with water, add 2 tablespoons of the salt and the potatoes, cover, and bring to a boil over high heat. Cook until just fork-tender but cooked through, 6 to 7 minutes.

2   While the potatoes cook, mix the mayonnaise, sour cream, scallions, parsley, tarragon, anchovies (if desired), vinegar, lime juice, remaining 1 teaspoon salt, and the black pepper together in a large bowl.

3   Drain the potatoes well and add them to the bowl; toss with the dressing. Season to taste with salt and black pepper. Let stand for 15 minutes at room temperature (as the salad loses its heat, it will absorb the dressing). Serve at room temperature, or cover and refrigerate for up to 2 days before serving.

CABBAGE AND LIME SALAD
WITH ROASTED PEANUTS

serves 6 · TIME: 2 hours resting, 15 minutes preparation

Winter salads can be just as vibrant as June's blowsy, lazy salads, if you use a little creativity. Pretty "red" cabbage—more of a purple if you ask us—and green cabbage can be wilted with salt and combined into a confetti that we bulk up with ribbons of tender baby spinach, and then toss with a simple peanut and cumin dressing. The resulting slaw-salad has a brisk tropical feel from the fresh bits of lime (a perfect winter fruit if ever there was one) and a satisfying crunch. The cabbages can be speedily shredded with a food processor, and can be salted a day ahead of time for quick assembly the day you intend to serve the salad. We recommend pairing it with Mushroom and Okra Purloo (page 186) and Skirt Steak with Parsley Sauce (page 171).

½ small red cabbage, trimmed, cored, and shredded (about 6 cups)

½ small green cabbage, trimmed, cored, and shredded (about 6 cups)

1 tablespoon kosher salt, plus more to taste

1 bunch fresh baby spinach, stemmed and cut into ½-inch-wide ribbons (about 4 cups, loosely packed)

1 lime, segmented (see Segmenting Citrus, page 130)

¼ cup fresh lime juice (from about 2 small limes)

1 tablespoon Dijon or other salty prepared mustard

½ teaspoon ground cumin

¼ cup plus 1 tablespoon peanut oil

½ cup roasted unsalted peanuts, coarsely chopped

Freshly ground black pepper

1   In a large bowl, toss the shredded red and green cabbage with the salt. Transfer the cabbage to a colander, place it over the bowl, and let it drain for 2 hours.

2   Discard the salty water in the bowl. Rinse and dry the bowl, and return the cabbage to it. (Covered, salt-wilted cabbage will keep for a couple days in the fridge.)

3   Add the spinach to the cabbage and scatter the lime segments over the top. In a medium bowl, whisk the lime juice, mustard, and cumin together. Add the peanut oil in a thin stream, whisking constantly until the ingredients are thoroughly emulsified. Toss the salad with the dressing and add the roasted peanuts. Season to taste with salt and black pepper. This salad is best served immediately, but leftovers will keep for a day or two in the refrigerator.

segmenting citrus ⋯ We love perfect segments of citrus that contain only pulp—no peel, no pith, not even the thin membrane that articulates the sections of fruit. Some people refer to these segments as "supremes," and they truly *are* supreme in recipes—whenever we want a blast of pure citrus juice in a solid, textural form. They are typically made from grapefruit and oranges for fruit salads, but we make them from limes and lemons too because they work so well in salad and shellfish preparations. They're easy to prepare: Simply trim off the bottom and top of the fruit with a knife so that you have a flat surface upon which to rest it. At the stem end, you see a cross-section of the fruit that reveals where the citrus pulp meets the pith (or skin). Begin peeling the fruit by placing the tip of a sharp knife just inside the border where the pith meets the pulp and slicing down with a firm, clean stroke, following the curvature of the fruit. Repeat until the entire fruit has been peeled. Then, over a bowl or wide board to catch all the juice, gently cut out the segments of pulp with a sharp knife by cutting toward the core, as close as possible to the membranes that separate the segments. Once you've extracted all the citrus supremes, squeeze the membranes to release any remaining juice and then discard the membranes.

CARROT AND TURNIP SLAW WITH DILL

serves 4 to 6 • TIME: 10 minutes preparation, 1 hour resting

We're crazy about carrot slaws—they're cool and nutritious, they provide a ton of color and flavor on the plate, and they're perfect for the summer months in Charleston, when the last thing on our minds is lighting up the stove. We toss a healthy dose of dill into the mix here, and not just because it's in the same botanical family as carrots: dill spices up and complements any root vegetable's sweetness, and it is always plentiful in the summer garden. Dill conveniently reseeds itself every year—hence its reputation as a weed. For the record, cumin (used to season this slaw) is also in the same family, Apiaceae, along with fennel, chervil, coriander, parsley, and caraway.

Serve generous helpings of carrot and turnip slaw in place of any salad, with Pan-Fried Trout with Lemon and Herb Stuffing (page 177), or with Shrimp and Deviled-Egg Salad Rolls (page 183). It's also a terrific garnish for grilled hot dogs and pulled-pork barbecue sandwiches.

Although you could use a box grater to shred the carrots and turnips, a food processor will reduce your prep time dramatically.

1 pound medium carrots, trimmed, peeled, and grated	¼ cup red or white wine vinegar	½ teaspoon crushed dried red chile flakes
8 ounces white turnips, trimmed, peeled, and grated	2 tablespoons extra-virgin olive oil	1 teaspoon kosher salt, plus more to taste
2 tablespoons finely chopped fresh dill	¼ teaspoon ground cumin	½ teaspoon freshly ground black pepper, plus more to taste
	2 small cloves garlic, finely grated	

1 Combine the carrots, turnips, and dill in a large bowl and toss until thoroughly combined.

2 In a small bowl, whisk the vinegar with the olive oil, cumin, garlic, chile flakes, salt, and pepper. Pour the dressing over the slaw and toss until the slaw is evenly coated. Cover and let rest in the refrigerator for an hour, or for up to 2 days.

3 Just before serving, toss the slaw again, and season it to taste with salt and black pepper.

SNOW PEA AND CARROT SALAD
WITH GINGER DRESSING

serves 4 · TIME: 25 minutes

This stealthy salad is composed only of iceberg lettuce, shredded carrots, and thinly sliced snow peas. It may resemble something generic that you'd encounter on a lunch tray in a Japanese airport. But the dressing—made with a whole cucumber buzzed in the blender with fresh ginger juice—gives this salad an upbeat, invigorating flavor, a velvety texture, a peppery bite, and a melon-like sweetness using no sugar whatsoever. It's a jolt of refreshment any time your main course or other sides—Pimento-Cheese Potato Gratin (page 155), say, or Pork Tenderloins with Madeira and Fig Gravy (page 207)—are running rich.

6 ounces snow peas (about 2 large handfuls), blanched and thinly sliced	I head iceberg lettuce, trimmed and cored, sliced into ¼-inch-wide ribbons	I large (about 12-ounce) cucumber, peeled, seeded, and cut into chunks
8 ounces carrots (about 4 medium), peeled and coarsely shredded on a box grater	I teaspoon kosher salt, plus more to taste	3 tablespoons vegetable oil
	One 3-ounce piece of fresh ginger (about 4 inches long), peeled	2 tablespoons white wine vinegar

1 Toss the snow peas, carrots, and lettuce with ½ teaspoon of the salt in a large bowl until evenly combined.

2 Finely grate the ginger onto a clean cutting board, using a ginger grater or a Microplane (you can use the fine-gauge side of a box grater, but ginger fibers tend to be difficult to clean from it). Gather up the grated ginger and place it in a mound in the middle of a double thickness of paper towel. Pick up the corners of the paper towel and gently press the grated ginger over a small bowl to release the juice; you should have about 2 tablespoons. Pour the juice into the bowl of a food processor, and add the cucumber, vegetable oil, white wine vinegar, and remaining ½ teaspoon salt. Process until the dressing is smooth and thoroughly combined, about twenty 5-second pulses. (Covered, the dressing will keep for 2 days in the refrigerator.)

3 Pour the dressing over the salad and toss it with tongs or salad forks until the salad ingredients are evenly coated. Season to taste with salt, and serve.

notes on pitting avocados ⋯ Pitting an avocado requires some bladesmanship and simple know-how. First, cut the avocado in half lengthwise by holding its heel end in your palm, with the stem end resting just above your index finger; then, holding your knife so its blade is parallel to the ground, gently pierce the stem end, sawing the blade of the knife toward the pit. When you can feel that the blade of the knife has made contact with the pit, use the pit as a pivot, pulling the knife gently toward you and using your palm to push the fruit toward the blade to facilitate the cut. Once you've made a cut clean around the whole avocado, separate the halves by twisting one half of the fruit clockwise with one hand while you twist the other half counterclockwise. The halves should fall away easily, and one half will still contain the pit embedded in it. To extract the pit, set the avocado half on your cutting board with the pit facing up. Briskly whack your knife's blade into the pit so that it sinks in about ½ inch. Lift your knife, and if you've cut deep enough into the pit, the avocado half will lift with it. Then, with the hand that's not holding the knife, cradle the avocado in your palm and gently twist it. The pit will remain stuck to the knife, while the avocado half falls cleanly away.

ROASTED RED PEPPER AND CORN SALAD WITH TUNA

serves 4 · TIME: 10 minutes preparation, 15 minutes cooking

This simple salad packs maximum flavor because the vegetables—just two, red peppers and corn—get heat applied to them to bring out their flavor. We skillet-toast the corn the way we do okra (see page 125); letting it blister and brown, bringing out the smoky, gentle burnt-sugar character of corn grilled over a wood fire.

When we roast, peel, and dice the red peppers for this salad, we try to preserve as much of their juice as possible because it carries so much flavor. And we serve the salad over slices of avocado, which requires this small but key piece of strategy: wait until you're ready to serve the salad before cutting into the avocado, so it doesn't brown by the time the plates hit the table.

3 medium ears fresh corn (about 1 pound), husked

2 medium red bell peppers, or one 9-ounce jar high-quality store-bought roasted red peppers or piquillo peppers, drained

3 tablespoons fresh lemon juice (from 1 large lemon)

1 teaspoon kosher salt, plus more to taste

¼ cup extra-virgin olive oil

6 ounces solid white canned albacore tuna (preferably packed in water), drained

Freshly ground black pepper

1 ripe Hass avocado

1 Cut the corn kernels from the cobs; you should have about 1½ cups. Toast the corn in a dry skillet or sauté pan over medium-high heat, stirring with a wooden spoon, until the kernels just begin to brown in patches, about 8 minutes. Reserve the corn in the skillet, off the heat.

2 If you are using fresh bell peppers, turn on the broiler. Put the peppers in a dry flameproof skillet or broiling pan, and slide it under the broiler. Roast until the skin blackens on the side facing up, 3 to 5 minutes. Using tongs, turn the peppers so that an unblackened side faces up, and repeat. Continue until the skin of the

(recipe continues)

peppers is blackened on all sides. Place the peppers in a medium bowl, cover, and let steam for 5 minutes as they cool. Uncover the bowl. When the peppers are cool enough to handle, pull off their stems and discard them, and upend each pepper over the bowl so that any juice runs into it.

3   At this point, the process is the same whether you're using fresh or jarred peppers: Transfer the peppers to a cutting board, remove the blackened skin with your fingers, and discard it. Using a paring knife, cut open the peppers, remove the seeds, and discard them. (Jarred peppers tend to have just a few spots of black skin and a few errant seeds.) Cut the roasted pepper flesh into medium dice; you should have about 1½ cups. Strain out any stray seeds that may be in the red pepper juice in the bowl, and then add the diced red pepper to the bowl. Add the corn and toss until the ingredients are evenly combined.

4   In a small bowl, whisk the lemon juice with the salt and olive oil. Add the tuna, crumbling it to large flakes as you add it, and stir to coat the tuna with the dressing. Add the dressed tuna to the corn mixture and toss gently until the ingredients are thoroughly combined. Season to taste with salt and black pepper.

5   Slice the avocado in half lengthwise and extract the pit (see Notes on Pitting Avocados, page 134). Peel each avocado half and place it, flat side down, on your cutting board. Cut each half on the bias into slices ¼ inch thick. Divide the avocado slices among 4 small salad plates, fanning them around the edge of each plate. Place a scoop of the salad in the center of the plate, and garnish with a grind of black pepper. Serve immediately.

CURRIED NEW POTATO SALAD

serves 4 · TIME: **30 minutes**

We've met few potato salads we didn't love. Still, that doesn't stop us from trying to perfect them. Our take on the classic mayonnaise-based new-potato salad distinguishes itself from others you might have sampled in a number of ways: First, we break the salad down to size, cutting the potatoes into small hash-size dice so there's more surface area for the delicious dressing to cling to. It's as easy to eat as creamed corn. Second, the dressing gets a tangy kick from a trifecta of pickle relish, lemon juice, and white wine vinegar—the combination is much tastier than any two ingredients. Third, we mix some buttermilk in with the mayonnaise to cut the richness of the mayo. Ever yearned for a refreshing potato salad? This one's it.

True, you have to invest a few extra minutes to cut the potatoes small, but you can bet your sack of potatoes it's worth it.

5 teaspoons kosher salt, plus more to taste	¼ cup pickle relish or finely diced pickles	2 ribs celery, peeled and finely diced (1 cup)
2½ pounds small red potatoes, cut into ½-inch dice	Juice of 1 large lemon	1 cup thinly sliced scallions (white and green parts)
½ cup high-quality store-bought mayonnaise, such as Hellmann's or Duke's	1 tablespoon white wine vinegar or distilled white vinegar	Freshly ground black pepper
¼ cup whole or lowfat buttermilk	1 teaspoon curry powder or garam masala, plus more to taste	

1   Put 6 cups water, 4½ teaspoons of the salt, and the potatoes in a large saucepan, cover, and bring to a boil over high heat. Cook until the potatoes are just fork-tender, about 3 minutes. Remove from the heat and let sit in the hot water for 10 minutes while you prepare the dressing.

2   In a large salad bowl, whisk the mayonnaise with the buttermilk, pickle relish, lemon juice, vinegar, curry powder, and ½ teaspoon of the salt.

3   Drain the potatoes in a colander and run them under cold running water to cool. Shake off the excess water, and transfer the potatoes to the bowl containing the dressing. Add the celery and scallions, and toss until evenly coated with the dressing. Serve immediately, or cover and refrigerate until ready to serve (but not more than 2 days).

4   Before serving, season to taste with salt, curry powder, and black pepper.

FIELD PEA SALAD WITH
GINGERED BEETS AND LEMON

serves 4 · TIME: 20 minutes preparation, 20 minutes to 1 hour simmering

Fresh field peas are an indulgence of high summer, when farmers markets throughout the South are brimming with bags of shelled peas. Since field peas are removed by hand from their slender pods, they tend to be costly. If you've ever tasted a fresh field pea's lively bean flavor, you'll know they're worth it. But since their season is so short, and because we crave field peas year-round, we often turn to the dried varieties, which are a slightly different experience but every bit as valuable, with deep, soulful flavor, mellower and less sweet than the fresh. They are also dirt cheap and widely available. They do take a little longer to cook, but that's no hurdle for us.

This is a super-hearty salad that you can eat on the go as a complete meal, or with a simple two-egg omelet for a satisfying lunch. We temper the earthy sweetness of the beets and peas with lemon, ginger, and a generous handful of chopped scallions.

4 teaspoons kosher salt, plus more to taste	1 pound fresh red beets, peeled, trimmed, and cut into small dice (2½ to 3 cups)	⅓ cup grapeseed, peanut, vegetable, or mild olive oil
1 pound fresh or 8 ounces dried shelled field peas, such as red cowpeas, lady peas, pink-eyes, black-eyes, purple hulls, crowders, or zippers	One 3-ounce piece of fresh ginger (about 4 inches long), peeled	1 bunch scallions (white and green parts), chopped (¾ cup)
	2 tablespoons fresh lemon juice	½ teaspoon freshly ground black pepper
	1 teaspoon Dijon mustard	

1   Pour 2½ quarts water into a heavy-bottomed 4-quart stockpot, add 2½ teaspoons of the salt, and bring to a boil. Rinse the field peas in a strainer or colander, and add them to the boiling water. Cook until the peas are tender, maintaining the level of the cooking water just above the peas, about 20 minutes if you're using fresh field peas and 1 hour if using dried.

2   While the peas cook, pour 1 quart water into a small saucepan, add 1 teaspoon of the salt, and bring to a boil. Add the beets and cook until tender, about 15 minutes. Drain, and run them under cold tap water to cool. Then arrange the beets in a single layer on paper towels spread across a cutting board, and let them dry while the peas finish cooking.

(recipe continues)

3   Grate the ginger onto a cutting board, using a ginger grater or a Micro-plane. Set aside ½ teaspoon of the grated ginger. Gather the rest of the grated ginger and place it in a mound in the middle of a double thickness of paper towel. Pick up the corners of the paper towel and gently press the grated ginger over a small bowl to extract the juice; you should have about 2 tablespoons. Pour the ginger juice into a large bowl and add the lemon juice, mustard, and remaining ½ teaspoon salt. Drizzle in the oil, whisking constantly until the dressing is emulsified.

4   Drain the peas in a strainer and run them under cold tap water to cool; you should have about 3 cups cooked field peas. Shake the strainer to get rid of excess water. Add the peas and the reserved grated ginger to the dressing, and toss to coat. Add the beets and scallions, and toss gently. Season to taste with salt and the pepper. (Covered, the salad will keep in the refrigerator for 3 days.)

RED RICE SALAD

Tomatoes, rice, and a nice dose of smoky sausage combine to make the soulful classic southern side dish called red rice, often served alongside fried fish and hush puppies and on barbecue buffets. Last summer, finding ourselves with a surplus of cooked white rice and some gorgeous tomatoes, we decided to chill out the dish we know and love, and to place it more in a cold salad frame of mind. But we insisted on preserving the wonderful sour-and-sweet tomato inflection of the original.

The method we settled on is super-easy and squeezes every drop of flavor from the tomatoes we have on hand—even generic supermarket tomatoes come out tasting great in this recipe. Tomato water, from the seed cavities, is blended into a basic Dijon mustard vinaigrette, which lightly glazes the rice. If possible, make this a day or half a day in advance so the rice really absorbs the flavor of the tomatoes, as well as the basil and chives that season this salad bright.

1 pound plum or vine-ripened tomatoes (about 5 plum tomatoes), peeled	¼ cup chopped fresh chives	½ teaspoon kosher salt, plus more to taste
3 cups cooked white rice (from 1 cup uncooked)	¼ cup chopped fresh basil	¼ cup extra-virgin olive oil
	1 tablespoon Dijon mustard	
	1 tablespoon plus 1 teaspoon red wine vinegar	

1 Set a strainer over a small bowl. Core the tomatoes, cut them in half widthwise, and using your pinkie finger, tease the seeds out of the cavities, letting them drop into the strainer. Tap the rim of the strainer against your palm for 30 seconds, until most of the flavorful gel clinging to the seeds dissolves and drips into the bowl. Cover and refrigerate the tomato water; you should have about ¼ cup. Discard the seeds.

2 Chop the tomatoes into ½-inch dice, and toss them in a bowl with the rice, chives, and basil. Cover with plastic wrap and allow the flavors to meld in the refrigerator for at least 30 minutes, or for up to 24 hours.

3 In a small bowl, whisk together the reserved tomato water, mustard, vinegar, and salt. Add the olive oil in a thin stream, whisking constantly until the ingredients are thoroughly emulsified. Toss the dressing gently with the rice mixture. Serve cold or at room temperature. (Covered, the salad will keep in the refrigerator for 3 days.)

hot sides

Home cooks generally—and food writers in their bunny slippers in particular—seem to love dreaming up new ways to make the most familiar vegetables (potatoes, green beans, carrots, to name a few) seem less dreary and more unique.

We've focused much of our creative energy recently on making our hot side dishes sing, and not just for the challenge it presents, but to give ourselves the utmost flexibility when it comes to composing meals during a typical week. A simple hot side dish like Lemon-Glazed Sweet Potatoes, page 151, works wonderfully alongside any roasted protein, but a side like Pimento-Cheese Potato Gratin, page 155, is rich enough and dazzling enough as a meal in itself, when served with a fresh salad of lettuces or spinach.

There are some tantalizing tweaks in this chapter, like our spin on collards, which we blitz with spicy sausage and poblano peppers (page 146), or the silky, rich cauliflower mash seasoned with the sultry perfume of wood smoke (page 166). We turned a few pantry staples—frozen sweet peas, rice, red chile flakes—into a Hoppin' John variant that's ridiculously easy, good for you (and your wallet), and truly good eating.

Much of the art of the vegetable side dish is attained through trial and error, finding the grace notes that work best. We tried dozens of variations to discover that tarragon works beautifully with braised carrots, mint is perfect with a mix of root vegetables, and toasted sesame seeds (what we call "benne" in Charleston) are fantastic paired with the subtle sweetness of baked squash.

SQUASH HALF-MOONS WITH BUTTER, SESAME, AND SALT (PAGE 145)

RECIPES

Squash Half-Moons with Butter, Sesame,
and Salt

Collard Greens with Poblano Chiles
and Chorizo

Skillet Green Beans with Orange

Spinach with Collards Seasoning

Lemon-Glazed Sweet Potatoes

Pimento-Cheese Potato Gratin

Toasted Rice and Peas "Hoppin' John"

Roasted Parsnips with Mint

Roasted New Potatoes with Country
Ham and Chiles

Braised Carrots with Tarragon and Lime

Smoked Cauliflower

Roasted Zucchini with Toasted Pecans
and Lemon

SQUASH HALF-MOONS WITH BUTTER, SESAME, AND SALT

serves 6 • TIME: **40 minutes**

Dad's acorn squash (halves roasted with a pat of butter, a squeeze of lemon, and some salt in the middle) was one of the highlights of the winter season, and though it would be hard to improve on that, we've discovered a few tricks that elevate the dish to something we're proud to serve at a midwinter dinner party or a holiday feast. Toasted sesame seeds sprinkled over the top, and warm spices blended into the melted butter, add some nutty intrigue and complement the flavor of the squash beautifully.

8 tablespoons (1 stick) unsalted butter	4 teaspoons ground cinnamon, garam masala, curry powder, or your own blend of wintery spices	Two 1½-pound acorn or kabocha squash 2 teaspoons kosher salt 2 teaspoons sesame seeds

1   Heat the oven to 425°F, with a rack positioned in the middle of the oven.

2   Heat the butter in a small skillet over medium heat. When the froth on the butter begins to subside, thoroughly whisk in the cinnamon or other spices. Remove from the heat.

3   Cut each squash in half lengthwise and scoop out the seeds. Then slice each half lengthwise into 3 half-moon-shaped slices of roughly equal size. You should have 12 wedges total.

4   Place the squash half-moons, flesh side up, on a roasting pan or baking sheet, baste them with the spiced butter and season them with 1 teaspoon of the salt. Bake for about 35 minutes, or until the squash begins to brown at the upper corners and yields easily to a knife.

5   While the squash bakes, heat a dry skillet over high heat. Add the sesame seeds and toast them, stirring them occasionally, until you just notice their color beginning to darken, 2 to 3 minutes. Transfer the sesame seeds to a small bowl and set aside.

6   When the squash is ready, reheat the butter until it's hot. Baste each squash slice with the spiced butter, and then sprinkle them generously with the toasted sesame seeds and the remaining 1 teaspoon salt. Serve immediately.

COLLARD GREENS WITH POBLANO CHILES AND CHORIZO

serves 4 • TIME: 5 minutes preparation, 15 minutes cooking

We've always enjoyed cooking with fresh hot chiles, but we tended to use them simply as seasoning—a mere accent—until the summer of 2004, when we met Erik Lopez. At the time, Lopez was the 25-year-old kitchen steward of the four-star New York restaurant Daniel, and we were reporting our first "The Industry" column for the *New York Times.* We love interviewing people with interesting jobs in the food industry, jobs that you may never have imagined existed.

We shadowed Lopez through 3 long days as he hustled around the network of basement kitchens and sub-basement storerooms. The best part of his day—and ours, as it turned out—was the "family meal," the staff meal typically prepared on the fly from whatever happens to be available. Often, for the Mexican-born members of the kitchen staff, that meant a simple salad of equal parts raw onion, tomato, avocado, and jalapeño, dressed with lime juice. The chile in the salad was treated not as an accent, but as a vegetable in its own right, and while the salad was spicy (raw onion is hot, too!), it also had an undeniably fantastic flavor. It encouraged us to get bold with our chiles when the mood strikes, to treat them as a vegetable the same way we do an eggplant or a mushroom. If you choose chiles that are tolerably hot, you'll add new dimensions to all sorts of dishes.

Dark poblanos often fit the bill because they tend to be milder than many jalapeños and they've got terrific green-pepper flavor. In this adaptation of the easy collard greens recipe we make on weeknights, poblano strips are charred in the pan with the chorizo, giving the dish a depth and an exoticism rarely found in typical collard greens recipes.

2 teaspoons peanut or canola oil

8 ounces fresh chorizo (see Chorizo Shopping Notes, opposite), casings removed, cut into roughly 1-inch pieces; or 4 ounces cured chorizo, kielbasa, or other smoked sausage, finely diced

3 poblano chiles, seeded and sliced into thin 2- to 3-inch strips (about 3 cups)

2 teaspoons finely chopped garlic

1½ pounds collard greens (about 1 bunch), ribs removed, leaves thinly sliced (1 packed quart)

1 teaspoon kosher salt, plus more to taste

2 tablespoons red wine vinegar

1 Pour the oil into a 12-inch skillet or sauté pan set over high heat, and when it shimmers, add the chorizo. Cook, chopping up the (fresh) sausage with the back of a spoon, until the sausage has rendered most of its fat, about 2 minutes. Add the poblanos, and continue to cook until they have softened slightly and the chorizo is cooked through, about 4 minutes.

2 Add the garlic, half the collards, the salt, and 2 tablespoons water to the skillet. Cook, turning the collards with tongs and adding more greens as those in the pan wilt, until all the collards are in the skillet. Continue to cook until the collards have softened and become dark green, about 6 minutes. Add the vinegar and continue to cook the collards, turning them occasionally, until the vinegar has completely evaporated and the pan is dry, about 3 minutes more. Season to taste with salt, if necessary, and divide the collards, poblanos, and chorizo among 4 warm serving plates. Serve immediately.

chorizo shopping notes ··· Chorizo, a smoked-paprika-spiked pork sausage with origins in Spain and Portugal, is most commonly found in American markets as a dry-cured (fully cooked) packaged sausage imported from Spain or Mexico. But it can be also be found as a fresh sausage at some butchers, and we prefer the latter variety in these collards if it's available. Cut from their casings, the sausages crumble as they cook, distributing tasty little bits of flavor throughout the collard greens and offering a more integrated taste experience. But the cured variety is no slouch, and in fact tends to be a more intense experience altogether (similar to the way dried herbs have a more powerful flavor than fresh). And the cured variety holds its shape when cooked, so it tends to be a more muscular, toothsome presence in a dish. For that reason, if you can't find fresh chorizo, use half the quantity of a cured chorizo—or another smoky dry-cured sausage—in this recipe.

SKILLET GREEN BEANS WITH ORANGE

serves 4 • TIME: 10 minutes preparation, 10 minutes cooking

The slender, tender French *haricots verts* that have emerged in upscale food markets in recent years bear no resemblance to the leathery-skinned, stout green beans our parents grew when we were kids, the kind that seemed suited only to long simmering in a pot with a chunk of really good bacon. In this recipe, we "skillet-toast" those fat beans, which adds a charred, smoky dimension to them, transforming even the toughest beans—which, truth be told, is the kind we find most often in the precincts of the U.S. we inhabit—into something as addictively delicious as salted popcorn.

Serve these beans with Pimento-Cheese Potato Gratin (page 155) and Skirt Steak with Parsley Sauce (page 171), and you have a well-rounded, knockout menu that takes only an hour to prepare.

I large navel orange	¾ teaspoon kosher salt, plus more to taste	2 tablespoons extra-virgin olive oil
2 teaspoons canola oil	I tablespoon white wine vinegar, champagne vinegar, or rice vinegar	Freshly ground black pepper
I pound green beans, ends trimmed		

1 Finely grate the zest of the orange, and reserve it. Segment the orange (see Segmenting Citrus, page 130), and keep the sections and juice in a bowl.

2 In a large cast-iron skillet or sauté pan, heat the canola oil over high heat, swirling it around the pan so it coats the bottom thinly and evenly. When the oil begins to smoke, add the beans (in batches, if necessary—don't crowd the pan) and scatter ½ teaspoon of the salt over them. Cook, stirring only every 1½ to 2 minutes, until the beans are half blistered and blackened, about 8 minutes. Transfer the beans to a serving platter or bowl. Lift the orange segments out of their juice (reserve the juice), and scatter them over the beans. Sprinkle ¼ teaspoon of the orange zest over the beans and oranges.

garnish it rich

* * *

With pieces of Buttermilk Fresh Cheese (page 93) crumbled over the beans just before serving.

3 Add the vinegar, olive oil, and remaining ¼ teaspoon salt to the bowl of orange juice, and whisk until thoroughly combined. Pour the dressing over the beans. Toss, and season to taste with salt, black pepper, and the remaining orange zest.

SPINACH WITH COLLARDS SEASONING

serves 4 • TIME: 5 minutes preparation, 15 minutes cooking

As much as we love sturdy greens like collard, mustard, and turnip, they take a while to wash and de-rib and chop. And even if you like them al dente, as we do, they take longer to cook than fresh spinach. This is a recipe that takes all the seasonings we love in our recipes for sturdy greens—smoked bacon, vinegar, crushed red pepper, and a smidgen of sugar—and transposes them to fresh spinach, a vegetable that takes considerably less time to clean, trim, and cook. Don't get us wrong: we love our collards, but sometimes you need a dish in the arsenal that hits all the pleasure points collards do but takes only 20 minutes to make.

---

2 ounces slab bacon, or 2 strips thick-cut bacon, finely diced

2 tablespoons apple cider vinegar or red wine vinegar

½ teaspoon crushed dried red chile flakes

½ teaspoon kosher salt

¼ teaspoon sugar

1¼ pounds fresh spinach, stems trimmed

Scatter the bacon in a skillet set over medium-high heat and cook, stirring, until just browned, about 4 minutes. Add 2 tablespoons water and the vinegar, chile flakes, salt, and sugar. Simmer until slightly reduced, about 1 minute. Add the spinach by handfuls, tossing the leaves in the skillet and adding more as they wilt, until all the spinach has wilted, about 4 minutes. Serve immediately.

LEMON-GLAZED SWEET POTATOES

serves 4 • TIME: 5 minutes preparation, 50 minutes cooking

n Van Zandt County, Texas, sweet potatoes have been the king commodity for nearly fifty years. We journeyed to the heart of the county, about 50 miles east of Dallas, to interview a sweet-potato farming family—Dale Smith, his wife, Roma, and their son, Sheb—and we got a seed-to-market perspective on raising these curious orange torpedoes. Among other interesting facts, we learned that sweet potato vines can be cut into short segments and replanted, and that the wild hogs in east Texas wreak so much havoc on the crop, tearing up the sandy soil to get to the nutritious tubers, that if you bring the ears of a hog you've killed to the county extension agent, he'll give you $7 cash.

When we returned from touring the fields, Roma offered us inch-thick slices of roasted sweet potato from a platter. They were naked—no salt, no nothing—and had just come from the oven. She explained that when she was a child, her mother had served these to her and her siblings as an afternoon snack. The disks were as delicious as candy—though not nearly as sweet, fortunately—and it drove home the point that when it comes to fresh vegetables, sometimes less is more.

This simple, light version of the candied whipped sweet potatoes we encounter around the holidays is a side dish for everyday. We've dispensed with the frozen orange juice concentrate, the burnt marshmallow, the vanilla extract, and most of the sugar and butter, but trust us: there's nothing ascetic about these glazed sweet potatoes. They're a celebration of sweet potatoes' essential minerally, earthy flavor. They go particularly well with a curry-flavored main dish, such as a country captain, or with a fresh roasted ham of wild boar, if you're really entertaining the sweet potato spirit.

---

2 pounds sweet potatoes (about 3 medium potatoes)	2 tablespoons dark brown sugar	⅛ teaspoon ground cinnamon
1 tablespoon unsalted butter	½ cup fresh lemon juice (from about 3 lemons)	⅛ teaspoon kosher salt

---

(recipe continues)

1   Heat the oven to 325°F.

2   Peel the sweet potatoes and cut them into 1-inch-thick slices. Grease a 9-x-13-inch baking dish with the butter. Arrange the sweet potato disks in a single layer in the pan. Mix the brown sugar, lemon juice, cinnamon, and salt in a small bowl, and pour the glaze mixture evenly over the potatoes.

garnish it rich

. . .

With dollops of sour cream whipped with curry powder or garam masala and kosher salt to taste.

3   Cover the baking dish with aluminum foil, and bake until the potatoes are fork-tender, about 45 minutes. Remove the foil and cook for about 5 more minutes, until the glaze has thickened and become syrupy. Serve immediately. (The glazed sweet potatoes can be cooked in advance, stored in the refrigerator, and reheated in a warm oven.)

PIMENTO-CHEESE POTATO GRATIN

serves 6 • TIME: 10 minutes preparation, 35 minutes cooking

Pimento cheese, sometimes called the South's "house pâté," is a simple cheese spread made with extra-sharp cheddar, mayonnaise, and diced roasted red peppers. It's a very mildly peppery blend straight from the midcentury, and it's delicious on celery sticks, sandwiches, and hamburgers.

We hosted two parties, one in New York and one in Charleston, for our first book (which contains two recipes for "P.C."). For the New York shindig, we booked a crack team of four kitchen-savvy transplanted southerners, and we all pitched in to make 1,800 pimento-cheese tea sandwiches over the course of two days.

All 1,800 sandwiches disappeared in the first twenty minutes of the party (that's 90 per minute!). One editor at a major food magazine was spotted with a stack of six in her hand, and later, wrapping more in napkins to stuff in her purse.

This recipe hit like a thunderclap—why not juice up a gratin with the peppery double hit of sweet roasted peppers and hot crushed red chile? We went into the test kitchen and developed this casserole that has dethroned our macaroni and cheese for the title of favorite cheesy dish in the house!

3 teaspoons salt, plus more to taste	3 shallots, finely diced (scant ½ cup)	One 9-ounce jar roasted red peppers or piquillo peppers, with their liquid
1½ pounds Yukon Gold potatoes, peeled and sliced into ¼-inch-thick rounds	¼ teaspoon crushed dried red chile flakes	8 ounces extra-sharp cheddar cheese, coarsely grated (about 2 cups)
¾ cup heavy cream	½ teaspoon freshly ground black pepper	

1 Heat the oven to 375°F, with racks positioned in the middle and the top third of the oven.

2 In a 3- to 4-quart stockpot, bring 2 quarts water and 2 teaspoons of the salt to a boil. Add the potatoes and cook for 10 minutes. Then drain, and set them aside.

3 Combine the cream, shallots, chile flakes, remaining 1 teaspoon salt, the black pepper, and 2 tablespoons of the liquid from the jar of roasted peppers in a small saucepan. Bring to a simmer and cook until the chile flakes have begun to stain the cream, about 2 minutes. Add half of the cheese and stir until it melts, about 1 minute. Remove the pan from the heat.

(recipe continues)

4   Layer roughly a third of the potatoes in a 6-cup baking dish, overlapping them slightly so that they fit in an even layer. Scatter half of the roasted peppers on top of the potatoes (cut up any peppers that have remained whole so that they lie flat), and repeat layering potatoes and peppers until all the peppers and potatoes have been used. Pour the cream mixture over the potatoes and peppers, and agitate the dish to distribute the liquid throughout. Cover with aluminum foil and bake on the middle rack for 15 minutes.

5   Uncover the dish, sprinkle the remaining cheese over the top, and place the dish on the top oven rack. Bake for 8 minutes, or until the cheese is bubbly and gently browned on top. Serve immediately.

TOASTED RICE AND PEAS "HOPPIN' JOHN"

serves 4 • TIME: **20 minutes**

This shorthand Hoppin' John is our ultimate weeknight convenience meal or side dish, whipped up from ingredients we almost always have on hand: basmati rice and frozen peas. What makes this recipe sing a more interesting tune (and what justifies our serving it to guests on occasion) is the first step: sautéing the rice in the pot with a little bit of oil to bring out an interesting toasty, popcorn-like flavor; the liquid is added only after the rice has been altered in this fashion. If you haven't tried it yet, you may discover yourself using this little trick every time you prepare a pot of rice. At first it may appear as crazy to you as it did to us when as little kids we noticed Mom heating rice in what appeared to be a dry pot.

What we later discovered, by reading Karen Hess and other food historians, is that the roots of this technique (and the tradition of cooking pieces of protein together with the rice in the pot) can be traced to ancient Mesopotamia. The path Hoppin' John most likely took to the American Southeast runs, across many centuries, through northern Africa, where the dish married rice with various types of beans. In the South Carolina Lowcountry, traditional twentieth-century Hoppin' John marries white rice with some variety of field pea, like black-eyed peas, cowpeas, or purple-hull peas, all of which are actually small beans.

We ponder this hallowed tradition as we unceremoniously dump a brick of frozen California-grown "English peas" (our legume of choice in this instance) into the intensely aromatic Southeast Asian rice variety called basmati (Louisiana-grown), and feel a bit sneaky. Hey, any way you slice it, rice and legumes are a great source of protein and terrific flavors.

What seems particularly illicit about our recipe is its efficiency: the peas cook in the pot of hot cooked rice during that extra 5 minutes that we always seem to need before dishing up—to assemble plates and cutlery, pour wine into glasses, and to rip off a few paper towel "napkins."

One 10-ounce package frozen English (garden) peas	½ teaspoon crushed dried red chile flakes (optional)	½ teaspoon flaky finishing salt, such as Maldon, or more to taste (see Notes on Finishing, page 159)
1 tablespoon bacon fat or olive oil	2 tablespoons extra-virgin olive oil, preferably a fancy finishing one (see Notes on Finishing, page 159)	
1 cup basmati rice (do not rinse)		½ teaspoon freshly ground black pepper

(recipe continues)

1   Remove the peas from the freezer.

2   Set a heavy 2-quart saucepan over medium-high heat for 1 minute; then add the bacon fat or olive oil and heat it for 1 minute. Add the rice, stirring it with a wooden spoon until the grains are all coated and shiny. Toast the rice, stirring it only occasionally, for 2 minutes, by which time a toasty popcorn aroma should be issuing from the pot (feel free to toast a minute longer if you wish).

3   Add 2 cups water and stir to evenly distribute the rice in the water. Once the water is simmering, turn the heat down to low, and cover the pan with the lid just slightly ajar for steam to escape. Simmer the rice for exactly 10 minutes.

4   Remove the pan from the heat and add the frozen peas and chile flakes, stirring to incorporate and breaking up any large clumps of peas. Cover the pan tightly, and allow it to sit for a full 5 minutes, off the heat, without peeking.

5   Add the olive oil, salt, and pepper, and stir once or twice to partially incorporate. Serve immediately.

notes on finishing ⋯ When we talk about "finishing" a dish, we're really talking about garnishing it. But somehow the word *garnish* implies an ingredient that's on the side, that's optional. We think the grace notes we typically garnish a dish with—olive oil, flaky salt, citrus zest—are important. They make wholesome food extraordinary, especially when you're cooking quickly and monastically to put nutrition on the table: a pot of rice, a plate of steamed vegetables.

And you need not spend a fortune in a gourmet store to finish food the way the pros do. Taste around the marketplace and settle on one top-notch olive oil and one salt that you really love, and get comfortable and happy with your zesting technique. Here's what we do:

OLIVE OIL We cook and make salad dressing with supermarket brands of olive oil. But for finishing a dish, we always have on hand one premium-quality extra-virgin oil with fruity, peppery flavor and a luminous green color for drizzling over foods. New York–based Fairway Market has oils from Italy, Spain, Mexico, and California at bargain prices; the $16 liter of one of our favorites, made from Arbequina olives that grow in Catalonia, lasts almost six months.

SALT Some years back, we wrote a story about salts from around the world, and we bought nearly $300 worth from India, Peru, Hawaii, and Denmark, to name a few. After sampling all those salts, and more since, we've never found a better or more versatile finishing salt than Maldon salt, harvested from the Blackwater River near Maldon, England. These thin, pyramidal crystals of salt have a gentle aquatic tang; a pinch is all that's required to bring out the flavor of a dish and add an appealing crunch. An 8½-ounce box of Maldon salt costs about $7 and typically lasts us eight months. It's available in most cookware stores.

CITRUS ZEST Citrus zest is an intensely flavorful finishing ingredient and it costs next to nothing. A fine-gauge Microplane grater is a cheap, wonderful tool for creating a shower of small flecks of orange zest—or hard cheese, nutmeg, or cinnamon for that matter—in a flash. The resulting zest will be so small, it will seem to disappear into a dish—especially those with dressings or oils—but will provide big flavor. If you don't have a Microplane grater and just can't tolerate another tool in the kitchen (or if you want the zest to add visual color to a dish), cut broad chips of zest (not the pith, just the very surface of the citrus skin) with a paring knife, then slice them into thin strips before scattering over your dish.

ROASTED PARSNIPS WITH MINT

serves 4 • TIME: **30 minutes**

Although gardeners mostly resent mint for its ability to take over the territory, we use so much in our cooking that it never has a chance to get very far (and unless we get a really hard freeze, it survives year-round in planters!).

We love mint. The flavor is so chlorophyllic, sweet, and sunny, it seems to promise good times ahead. In this recipe, mint transforms a sturdy autumnal root vegetable into something springlike.

We cut our parsnips into 2-inch "rods" for a couple reasons: they cook more quickly, and they're easier to eat. Serve yourself a generous portion on the first go-round because this dish disappears fast.

2 pounds parsnips or other sturdy root vegetables, such as turnips or rutabagas, trimmed

7 tablespoons extra-virgin olive oil

1 teaspoon kosher salt

¼ teaspoon freshly ground black pepper

1 bunch scallions (6 to 8 scallions), roots trimmed, white and green parts cut into 3-inch lengths

3 tablespoons red wine vinegar

2 tablespoons finely chopped shallot

1 clove garlic, minced

½ cup finely chopped fresh mint

1 Heat the oven to 400°F.

2 Peel the parsnips and cut them into 2- to 3-inch-long segments. Slice each piece lengthwise to make rods that are roughly ⅓ inch in diameter. (If using turnips or rutabagas, slice them crosswise into disks ⅓ inch thick, then cut them into pieces about 2 to 3 inches long and ⅓ inch wide.) Place the parsnips in a large baking pan, and add 2 tablespoons of the olive oil, ½ teaspoon of the salt, and the black pepper. Toss to combine. Roast, turning occasionally and adding the scallions after 15 minutes, until the parsnips are nicely browned and cooked through, about 25 minutes.

3 While the vegetables roast, make the mint dressing: In a small bowl, whisk the remaining 5 tablespoons olive oil with the vinegar, shallot, garlic, remaining ½ teaspoon salt, and the mint.

4 Transfer the roasted vegetables to a serving platter, spoon the dressing evenly over them, and serve.

ROASTED NEW POTATOES WITH COUNTRY HAM AND CHILES

serves 4 • TIME: 5 minutes preparation, 35 minutes cooking

We love crispy roasted potatoes, and this easy side dish hits all the southern comfort notes: salty, hammy, appetizingly spicy. Though perfectly wonderful with Gran's Flank Steak (page 202), these potatoes also put us in a breakfast state of mind: Heat up any leftovers on a plate and drape poached or sunny-side-up eggs over them. Yum!

1½ pounds small new potatoes, spots trimmed, quartered

2 tablespoons extra-virgin olive oil

1 tablespoon balsamic vinegar

½ teaspoon kosher salt

½ teaspoon freshly ground black pepper

6 to 8 ounces poblano chiles (about 2 large chiles)

4 ounces very thinly sliced uncooked country ham, prosciutto, or Serrano ham, cut into thin strips

1 Heat the oven to 425°F.

2 Scatter the potatoes in a 9-x-13-inch roasting pan, and drizzle the oil and the vinegar over them. Then sprinkle the salt and pepper over them, and toss with your hands until evenly coated. Roast for 10 minutes.

3 While the potatoes roast, stem and seed the poblanos. Cut them into strips 2 to 3 inches long and ¼ inch wide.

4 Remove the pan from the oven (leave the oven on). Sprinkle the poblanos among the potatoes, and toss together until the peppers are coated with the oil and seasonings. Return the pan to the oven and continue to roast until the potatoes and chiles are almost browned, about 25 minutes.

5 Transfer the potatoes and chiles to a serving platter. Sprinkle the ham over them, let it warm and melt slightly, and then serve.

country ham shopping notes ··· A country ham is the hind leg of a pig that's been cured in salt and sugar for a few weeks, hung in a smokehouse for another few weeks, and then aged for months. The process may take a year or more, during which time the ham loses almost a quarter of its weight, resulting in a super-concentrated turbo-ham much like Tyrolean speck (a smoked version of prosciutto).

The great majority of country hams sold and consumed in the South are cooked for a celebratory occasion or a holiday meal: they're first soaked in water, then boiled and baked. But these days, more and more ham fanciers are choosing to eat country ham uncooked and sliced paper-thin, in the manner of Spanish Serrano and Italian prosciutto. Southern country ham producers have even begun to market their hams as "Prosciutto-Style" or "American Prosciutto." This is a wonderful development for consumers, because a paper-thin slice of country ham is insanely flavorful and terrific in all kinds of preparations: wrapped around a piece of melon or cucumber, or tossed into an omelet, a soup, or a pasta.

A whole country ham can weigh from 10 to 19 pounds, and although it is worth every penny, purchasing one can be a commitment. Fortunately, producers sell pieces of uncooked country ham in 2- or 3-pound blocks. One of our favorite producers, Newsom's Country Hams in Princeton, Kentucky, sells a 3-pound pack for about $10 (shipping not included). When we get the pieces, we simply trim any skin with a kitchen knife, and then slice the flesh as thin as we possibly can. The slices won't be broad and beautiful the way they are when you slice from a whole ham, but they sure work for all the dishes we make.

A couple things to remember about buying whole country ham: *Don't be afraid of exterior mold:* A beneficial mold grows on country hams while they're in the smokehouse. And although it is benign, you should wash it off before slicing into your ham. Unless your health is at risk, due to age, illness, or pregnancy, *don't be afraid of the "Safe-Handling/Cooking Instructions"* sticker on a package of uncooked country ham, which would have you believe that you must cook the ham before you eat it. As long as you refrigerate the ham once the package is opened, it will keep for about a week or more, wrapped in waxed paper, in the refrigerator.

BRAISED CARROTS WITH TARRAGON AND LIME

serves 4 • TIME: 25 minutes

We loved the utilitarian cooked veggies we ate as kids—steamed carrots, steamed spinach, steamed broccoli—not for their own sake but because they were efficient carriers of melted butter! And we love 'em even more now that the vegetables themselves interest us.

These carrots are no more difficult than the steamed-with-butter variety, yet they have a playful tartness to them, and a depth of flavor that will jolt the kid in you awake. We braise the carrots briefly in white wine, scatter them with fresh tarragon and a squeeze of fresh lime juice, and then toss the carrots with crunchy-sweet caramelized onions and a dusting of lime zest.

Serve these carrots with straightforward main dishes like broiled pork chops, Smoked Trout (page 198), or Easy Chicken and Dumplings (page 181).

---

1 teaspoon extra-virgin olive oil

1 large (8-ounce) white onion, thinly sliced

½ teaspoon kosher salt, plus more to taste

2 pounds carrots, peeled and cut into rods about 2 to 3 inches long and ⅓ inch thick

½ cup full-flavored dry white wine, such as Sauvignon Blanc, Viognier, or unoaked Chardonnay

¼ teaspoon freshly ground black pepper, plus more to taste

Leaves from 3 sprigs fresh tarragon (about 2 tablespoons)

Grated zest and juice of ½ lime

---

1 Heat the olive oil in a large skillet over high heat until it begins to smoke. Add the onion slices, and spread them around in an even layer. Season with ¼ teaspoon of the salt. Cook, stirring at 2 minute intervals, until browned, about 8 minutes. Transfer the onions to a medium bowl.

2 Add the carrots and wine to the same skillet, and sprinkle with the remaining ¼ teaspoon salt and the black pepper. Cover and cook until the carrots are tender, about 6 minutes. Uncover the skillet, add the tarragon, and continue to cook until the liquid is almost all evaporated, about 2 minutes. Add the lime juice and reserved onions, and toss together. Season to taste with salt and black pepper, and serve warm with a small amount of lime zest scattered over each serving.

garnish it rich

• • •

With pieces of Buttermilk Fresh Cheese (page 93) broken over the carrots.

SMOKED CAULIFLOWER

serves 4 • TIME: 5 minutes preparation, 20 minutes cooking

Wylie Dufresne of the New York restaurant wd-50, one of this country's foremost avant-garde chefs, turned us onto the stovetop smoker's genius and simplicity (see Notes on Successful Stovetop Smoking, page 98). We were reporting a story about whether two flounders like us could replicate in our home kitchen the sort of groundbreaking dishes Wylie (and compatriots like Ferran Adrià and Grant Achatz) cooks. One exception to the onerous nature of this cooking was Wylie's smoked mashed potatoes, which came together in a snap and sent us into the kitchen to experiment with smoking a wide range of vegetables.

Cauliflower tweaked with hickory smoke emerged a victor from our tests. It's an easy, and just slightly unconventional, hot side dish that's a superb partner for Skirt Steak with Parsley Sauce, page 171, and Grillades and Gravy, page 212.

I tablespoon kosher salt, plus more to taste	I cup whole or lowfat buttermilk	Freshly ground black pepper
One 2½-pound cauliflower, halved, cored, and cut into large florets	4 tablespoons unsalted butter, melted	

1 Pour 4 cups water into a 2-quart saucepan, and add the salt and cauliflower. Bring to a boil over high heat, and continue to cook until fork tender, 4 to 6 minutes. Drain the cauliflower.

2 Put 1 tablespoon hickory smoking chips in the center of a stovetop smoker pan, or in the center of a 9-x-13-inch steel or aluminum roasting pan. If using a smoker pan, place the drip tray and rack inside the pan, put the cauliflower pieces on the rack, and partially cover. If using a conventional roasting pan and rack, wrap the rack in aluminum foil and place it in the pan, layer the florets on the rack, and cover it with aluminum foil, crimping the edges tightly, but leaving one corner uncrimped.

3 Turn the burner to low and center the pan above it. When you see the first wisp of smoke rise from the smoker or pan, cover it completely and continue to smoke for just 3 minutes. Transfer the cauliflower to the bowl of a food processor or blender, add the buttermilk and the butter, and process until the mixture is a smooth puree. Transfer the cauliflower to a serving bowl and season to taste with salt and black pepper.

ROASTED ZUCCHINI WITH TOASTED PECANS AND LEMON

serves 4 • TIME: **25 minutes**

Z ucchini become so abundant in late summer you can't give them away. But we've learned a number of stellar ways to eat zucchini: we pickle them with onions to make a superb condiment and side dish (see Zucchini and Onion Pickles, page 74); we slice them thinly lengthwise and throw them on the grill; and we roast them to make this simple, crowd-pleasing side dish.

3 pounds green zucchini (about 4 large or 9 small)	1½ teaspoons kosher salt, plus more to taste	1½ tablespoons walnut oil
3 tablespoons extra-virgin olive oil	½ teaspoon freshly ground black pepper, plus more to taste	Grated zest and juice of 1 large lemon
3 teaspoons white wine vinegar	½ cup crushed pecans	Maldon salt (see Notes on Finishing, page 159)

1   Heat the oven to 425°F with a rack positioned in the middle of the oven.

2   Cut the zucchini in half lengthwise, and then cut the halves lengthwise in thirds, so that each zucchini yields 6 slender wedges of roughly equal size. Slice these crosswise into 2-inch pieces.

3   Place the zucchini in a large rimmed baking sheet and add 1½ tablespoons of the olive oil, 1½ teaspoons of the white wine vinegar, ¾ teaspoon of the salt, and the black pepper. Toss to combine. Arrange the zucchini, skin side down, on the sheet and roast 15 to 20 minutes for small zucchini (25 to 30 minutes for large ones), or until just beginning to brown. Place the pecans on a separate baking dish or small cookie sheet, and toast for the last 3 to 4 minutes of cooking time. The pecans will be done when fragrant and gently browned.

4   While the zucchini roast, whisk the walnut oil, 1½ tablespoons of the lemon juice, the remaining 1½ tablespoons olive oil, the remaining 1½ teaspoons vinegar, and the remaining ¾ teaspoon salt in a large bowl.

5   Add the zucchini to the dressing and toss to coat. (If you have time, let it marinate for 15 to 20 minutes, tossing it every 5 minutes or so.) Transfer the zucchini to a serving platter, scatter the pecans and lemon zest over the top, drizzle dressing from the bowl over the top, and sprinkle with Maldon salt.

main dishes

The main dish is often what sets dinner in motion. It's the romance in the meal, the interesting protein or culinary idea that propels us into the kitchen instead of toward the take-out counter.

It could begin with a glance at a plump, glisteningly white chicken at the farmers market, an exquisite ingredient that called out to us above the din. Other times, with no prompting at all, a craving (Butterbeans! Burgers! Crispy salmon skin!) hits. And appetizing recipes we read about in cookbooks and magazines are frequently motivational.

Once the main dish has been decided, the ideas for sides begin to unspool, kindled by recent experiences or tastes, things read or witnessed: a magazine article about a journey in southern India might inspire us to think of seasoning that chicken with cinnamon and cardamom; a container of leftover cheese grits in the door of the refrigerator might launch us toward a fried-grits-cake accompaniment. This is how dinner is negotiated most nights, as a collaboration between what we have on hand and what we want from the local store.

Whatever the circumstances, the best-designed main dishes (and most of the ones included here) can stand as meals in themselves, with a good balance of protein, vegetable, and starch. The simple Whole Roasted Chicken with Potatoes and Onions (page 193) comes with a side dish of delectable roasted veggies built in. Caesar Salad with Catfish "Croutons" (page 173) promotes a salad into a perfect lunch. A terrific dessert and a nice bottle of wine will transform these dishes into a memorable dinner that feels just a little bit indulgent.

SKIRT STEAK WITH PARSLEY SAUCE (PAGE 171)

SKIRT STEAK WITH PARSLEY SAUCE

serves 6 · TIME: 20 minutes

When we were growing up, our mom had two cravings: One was for ice cubes, which she would chew at night while reading in bed, a pint glass of cubes resting in the crook of an open hardback. The other was for parsley, which she ate ravenously, a bunch at a sitting. Both cravings are signs of a mild iron deficiency, which Mom cured simply by eating more red meat. But even then, she never lost her love of the green stuff and it somehow rubbed off on all her children. If you've read this far, you've noticed that we enjoy its sprightly vegetal rush in everything from Oyster Cocktail No. 1 (page 80) to Easy Ambrosia (page 122) to Green Goddess Potato Salad (page 126).

We eat this iron-rich dish almost once a week. Skirt steak comes from the diaphragm of a cow—a well-marbled cut that has a rich, meaty flavor and is quite thin, so it takes just a couple minutes to sear on each side. At the end of a punishing workday, this tender charred steak with its piquant vinegar-spiked parsley sauce is the perfect restorative.

---

2 pounds skirt steak, cut into 4 steaks, each about 8 inches long

3 teaspoons kosher salt

1 bunch (about 8 ounces) parsley, preferably flat-leaf (see Notes on Parsley, below), trimmed of its toughest stems

2 cloves garlic, chopped

½ teaspoon crushed dried red chile flakes

⅓ cup red wine vinegar

½ cup plus 1 tablespoon extra-virgin olive oil

1 teaspoon freshly ground black pepper

2 teaspoons canola oil

---

notes on parsley ··· Because this recipe calls for buzzing the parsley up in the processor, it doesn't matter whether you use flat-leaf (a.k.a. "Italian") parsley or the curly-leaf variety. But we tend always to buy flat-leaf parsley because we believe that (a) the enfolded leaves of curly-leaf parsley tend to trap dirt, requiring more vigor to clean them, (b) the prickly mouth-feel of curly-leaf parsley tends to mute parsley's wondrous and unique flavor, which is like the aroma of tomato plants growing in the hot late-summer sun, (c) curly-leaf parsley reminds us of rote plate garnishes that aren't really meant to be eaten, served at restaurants that aren't really trying. There. We've said it. We hate curly-leaf parsley.

(recipe continues)

1 Season the steaks on both sides with 2 teaspoons of the salt, and set them aside.

2 Stuff the parsley into the bowl of a food processor, and add the remaining 1 teaspoon salt, the garlic, and the chile flakes. Pulse several times, pausing to push toward the blade any parsley that sticks to the side of the processor bowl, until the parsley is thoroughly chopped. With the processor running, add the vinegar in a thin stream, followed by the olive oil; process until the mixture is just shy of smooth (it should be slightly toothsome). You should have about 1⅓ cups of parsley sauce. Reserve it in a small bowl.

3 Pat the steaks with paper towels to absorb any moisture on their surface, and season on both sides with the black pepper. Pour the canola oil into a 12-inch skillet or sauté pan set over high heat, tilting the pan around as it heats until the entire bottom is coated with a thin sheen of oil. When the oil begins to smoke, add the steaks in batches, taking care not to crowd them in the pan, and sear them until each side is nicely browned, 2½ to 3 minutes per side. Transfer the steaks to a cutting board and tent them loosely with aluminum foil. Let them rest for 5 minutes.

4 Slice the steaks across the grain into ¼-inch-wide slices. Divide the slices among 4 plates, and spoon the parsley sauce liberally over them. Serve immediately.

CAESAR SALAD WITH CATFISH "CROUTONS"

serves 4 · TIME: **30 minutes**

As coastal dwellers, we have so many saltwater delicacies in our markets—wreckfish, triggerfish, flounder—that we never really messed with freshwater creatures until we experienced catfish nirvana at the Taylor Grocery and Restaurant. Taylor, Mississippi, a dogleg in the road 8 miles southwest of Oxford, is the kind of place where you can end up in a pottery studio, two art galleries, and on the mayor's porch drinking bourbon in the 20 minutes or so it takes to get a table at the "Grocery." When you sit down inside the former railroad depot, you're served some of the best fried catfish on earth: a crispy-nutty-salty crust enveloping meltingly tender fish. "Eat or We Both Starve" is their motto.

With this recipe, we bring some Taylor mojo to the ubiquitous Chicken Caesar found on the menu of almost every casual restaurant, replacing the often insipid grilled chicken with nuggets of cornmeal-battered fried catfish. In fact, do this right now: call up some friends you haven't seen in a while and invite them for dinner tonight. Make this salad along with a bowl of Creamy Sweet-Onion Soup (page 106). These easy comforts, especially on a gloomy fall Wednesday, will light up the night.

CATFISH CROUTONS

1 pound catfish fillets (about 3 fillets), cut into 1-inch chunks

⅓ cup whole or lowfat buttermilk

½ cup sifted all-purpose flour

¼ cup white or yellow fine stone-ground cornmeal

2½ teaspoons kosher salt

1 teaspoon freshly ground black pepper

2 cups peanut oil

CAESAR SALAD

1 large head romaine lettuce, sliced crosswise into ¾-inch-wide strips

⅓ cup whole or lowfat buttermilk (preferably whole)

2 tablespoons high-quality store-bought mayonnaise, such as Hellmann's or Duke's

2 anchovy fillets, minced, or ½ teaspoon anchovy paste

1 tablespoon fresh lemon juice

1 clove garlic, finely grated

½ teaspoon kosher salt

Put the catfish pieces in a medium bowl, pour the buttermilk over them, and toss to coat. Pour the flour, cornmeal, salt, and black pepper into a gallon-size locking food storage bag, and shake it around to combine. Lift the catfish pieces from the buttermilk, place them in the bag, and turn the bag gently in your hands until the pieces are covered in the dredge.

(recipe continues)

2 Heat the oil in a large deep skillet until it reads 375°F on a deep-frying thermometer. Using a wide slotted spoon or a skimmer, transfer a batch of the catfish pieces to the hot oil. Fry the fish in batches, taking care not to crowd the skillet, turning the pieces once as they become golden-brown, about 2 minutes per side. Transfer the fried catfish to a plate lined with a paper towel.

3 Put the lettuce in a large salad bowl. In a small bowl, whisk the buttermilk, mayonnaise, anchovies, lemon juice, garlic, and salt together. Pour the dressing over the greens and toss with tongs to coat evenly.

4 Divide the salad among 4 luncheon plates or salad bowls, and then scatter the catfish croutons on top of the greens. Serve immediately.

NOTE If you happen not to be a catfish fancier, any firm, sweet white-fleshed fish that holds up to frying—whiting, tilapia, and cod are others—works perfectly in this recipe.

PAN-FRIED TROUT WITH LEMON AND HERB STUFFING

serves 2 · TIME: **20 minutes**

Being from the Atlantic coast, we're all about our fish, but we don't leave our love behind when we travel upstate to visit friends in Asheville, North Carolina, or Emerts Cove, Tennessee, or anywhere in casting distance of the rivers of the southern Appalachian mountains, really. We're crazy for the varieties of freshwater trout—like rainbow, brook, and brown trout—we find there. Whether the fish are wild or farmed, a delicate, flaky flesh and a lightly aquatic, slightly nutty flavor are the hallmarks of a good trout. These perfectly sized fish take best to simple techniques (see also Smoked Trout, page 198).

In this recipe, the stuffing we make for the trout is actually a bread salad, similar to a cornbread salad you might make with leftover cornbread—except here we use easy-to-find white bread, and we cut everything up fine so it hugs the fish on every forkful.

2 tablespoons sifted all-purpose flour	4 tablespoons (½ stick) unsalted butter	½ cup mixed fresh herbs such as dill, parsley, and mint
1¼ teaspoons kosher salt	1 large lemon, segmented (see Segmenting Citrus, page 130)	2 tablespoons extra-virgin olive oil
½ teaspoon freshly ground black pepper	2 slices white or whole wheat bread, toasted, crusts cut off, cut into fine dice	1 teaspoon white vinegar
2 rainbow, brook, or brown trout fillets (about 6 ounces each)		

1 In a small bowl mix together the flour, salt, and pepper. Sprinkle the mixture over both sides of the trout fillets until they're evenly coated.

2 Melt the butter in a medium cast-iron skillet over medium heat until the froth begins to subside. Place the fillets in the skillet, skin side down, and cook until the skin is alluringly browned (you'll be able to see the edge of the fillet browning), about 5 minutes. Turn the fillets over and cook with the flesh side down for about 3 minutes.

3 While the fillets are cooking, toss the lemon segments, diced toast, and herbs in a bowl. Dress with the olive oil and the vinegar, and reserve.

4 Place a dollop of the lemon-herb mixture on each plate, lay a fillet, skin side up, over it, and serve immediately.

CRISPY-SKIN SALMON
WITH BUTTERMILK-MINT SAUCE

serves 4 · TIME: 20 minutes

We ate a ton of salmon as kids—our parents loved to poach bone-in cross-cut steaks in white wine and lemon juice. And though we developed a keen taste for the fish, the gummy skin (easy enough to pull off) is not very appetizing, even to look at, and we lived in fear of swallowing a needle-sharp bone.

And then we ate fried salmon skin in Charleston, at Sushi Hiro on King Street, and what a deliciously salty-crispy treat that was! In this recipe, we broil a large, generously seasoned piece of boneless salmon fillet skin side up so it gets blistery and delicious. The buttermilk-mint sauce, slightly tangy and cool, is there to temper the rich salmon and to give it a simple, fresh, southern flavor.

½ cup chopped fresh mint (leaves from about 8 sprigs)

½ cup whole or lowfat buttermilk

½ cup sour cream

1 teaspoon kosher salt

3 teaspoons extra-virgin olive oil

1 pound skin-on salmon fillet

⅛ teaspoon freshly ground black pepper

---

bed it down!

· · ·

Serve the salmon on a bed of simply steamed fresh spinach.

1 Combine the mint, buttermilk, sour cream, and ½ teaspoon of the salt in a food processor or blender, and process until thoroughly combined. Transfer the sauce to a bowl and reserve.

2 Pour 2 teaspoons of the oil into a large cast-iron skillet or broiler pan, and position it underneath the broiler so the bottom of the pan is about 5 inches from the heat source. Turn the broiler on.

3 As the broiler and the pan heat up, score the salmon skin crosswise in three places, to roughly portion the fish into 4 pieces. Massage the remaining teaspoon of oil over the skin of the fish, and sprinkle it with the remaining ½ teaspoon salt and the black pepper.

4 When the oil in the skillet is smoking, lay the fillet, skin side up, in the pan and cook for 5½ minutes, or until the skin is blistery and charring and the salmon is medium-rare.

5 Cut the salmon into 4 portions and serve it skin side up, with spoonfuls of the buttermilk-mint sauce.

EASY CHICKEN AND DUMPLINGS

serves 4 • TIME: **35 minutes**

Many southern families have a "house recipe" for chicken and dumplings, and those recipes can vary dramatically from kitchen to kitchen. At the richer end of the spectrum are thick, gravy-like stews of braised legs and thighs with dumplings the size of large biscuits nestled among them; at the other end are thin-as-consommé soups with threads of pulled chicken and delicate, noodle-like "rolled" dumplings.

Our simple fresh version of chicken and dumplings aims toward the middle of that spectrum, a luxurious chicken-noodle soup that you can whip up in a flash on weeknights. It's also an impressive-looking composed dish, with medallions of chicken breast and homemade dumplings in a soul-warming, oniony chicken broth. We should point out that what we call "dumplings" others might recognize as pasta that's been rough-cut by hand, called *maltagliati* in Italy.

If homemade dumplings sounds like too much work for a weeknight, let us assure you: they take no more than 10 minutes (and you perform that work while the chicken heats up). The only tools you need are a rolling pin and a knife: no pastry blender, no biscuit cutter required. And this dough is very forgiving: if it gets sticky, simply dust flour on it and keep working.

One note: bring the broth and chicken to a simmer *verrrrry* slowly over low heat. This keeps the chicken from tightening up and becoming tough.

---

2 tablespoons unsalted butter	1½ pounds skinless boneless chicken breast halves, sliced on the bias into ⅓-inch-thick medallions	1 large egg, beaten
1 medium yellow onion, finely chopped (1 cup)		8 sprigs fresh flat-leaf parsley, large stems trimmed off
1¼ teaspoons kosher salt		
3 cups chicken broth	¾ cup sifted all-purpose flour, plus more for dusting	

---

1 Melt the butter in a medium sauté pan over medium heat. Add the onion and ¼ teaspoon of the salt. Sauté, stirring, until the onion is translucent but not browned, about 6 minutes. Turn the heat to low, add the broth and the chicken pieces, and very slowly bring to a gentle simmer, about 15 minutes.

2 While the chicken and broth heat up, make the dumplings: Using a fork, mix the flour and remaining 1 teaspoon salt in a large bowl until they're combined. Add the beaten egg and toss it with the flour mixture until it

(recipe continues)

comes together in a number of balls of varying sizes. With lightly oiled hands, gather these pieces together into a single ball and knead it against the side of the bowl, gathering any dry flour from the sides of the bowl. Turn the ball out onto a lightly floured cutting board and knead it several times, pushing the dough against the board with the palm of your hand. Divide the dough ball in half. Using a lightly floured rolling pin, roll out one of the balls on the board until it is ⅛ inch thick (if the pin sticks to the dough, scatter flour by ½ teaspoonfuls onto the flattened dough, spreading it out on the surface with your fingers). Cut the rolled-out dough into strips about ¾ inch wide and 4 inches long, and reserve. Repeat with the second ball of dough. Each half makes about 32 dumplings.

3   When the broth is simmering and the chicken is just opaque, gently remove the chicken pieces from the broth with tongs and set them aside. If there's lots of protein foam floating on the broth and it's bumming you out, pass the broth through a fine-mesh strainer, or a strainer lined with cheesecloth, and return the clarified broth to the pot. Bring the broth to a vigorous simmer, add the dumplings, and simmer until they're cooked through but tender, about 6 minutes.

4   Return the chicken to the pot and heat through to serving temperature, about 1 minute. Divide the chicken and dumplings among 4 bowls, submerge a couple sprigs of parsley in each bowl, and serve immediately.

VARIATION

easy chicken and lemon–black pepper dumplings Dress up your dumplings in a flash by adding a two-part aromatic hit of lemon and black pepper: mix 1 teaspoon freshly ground coarse black pepper and ½ teaspoon lemon zest into the bowl of salt and flour before adding the egg.

SHRIMP AND DEVILED-EGG SALAD ROLLS

serves 4 · TIME: **30 minutes**

Think of these rolls as the Lowcountry cousin to lobster rolls—those uber-decadent (and expensive!) sandwiches of lobster morsels dressed with mayonnaise, lemon juice, and diced celery that get served in roadside joints up and down the New England coast in the summer. The idea here is simple: it's a super-tasty deviled-egg salad with chopped shrimp folded in, loaded into a hot-dog bun, then garnished with bacon bits and scallions.

2½ teaspoons kosher salt, plus more to taste

1 pound headless large shell-on shrimp (26 to 30 per pound; see Notes on Deveining Shrimp, page 61, and Shrimp Shopping Notes, page 63)

6 large eggs

2 ounces slab bacon, or 2 strips thick-cut bacon, finely diced

¼ cup plus 2 tablespoons high-quality store-bought mayonnaise, such as Hellmann's or Duke's

1 tablespoon pepper-vinegar hot sauce, such as Tabasco

2 teaspoons Dijon mustard

Freshly ground black pepper

2 vine-ripened red tomatoes, cut into 8 slices total

4 leaves butter lettuce

4 top-loading hot-dog buns

2 scallions (white and green parts), finely sliced

1   Fill a large stockpot with about 2 quarts water and 2 teaspoons of the salt, and bring to a boil over high heat. Remove the pot from the heat, add the shrimp, and cook (off the heat) for 1 to 2 minutes, until the shrimp are pink-orange and slightly firm. Using a slotted spoon or a skimmer, transfer the shrimp to a colander. Rinse them under cold water until they are cool enough to handle.

2   Return the shrimp water to a boil, and then reduce the heat to low so the water simmers calmly. Add the eggs gently, lowering them to the bottom, two at a time, with a large ladle. Let the eggs cook at a simmer for exactly 14 minutes.

3   While the eggs cook, peel and chop the shrimp and put them in a large bowl. Sauté the bacon in a skillet over medium-high heat until it is firm and just turning golden brown, 4 to 5 minutes. Transfer the bacon to a paper towel to drain.

4   When the eggs are done, transfer them to a strainer and rinse under cold water until they're cool enough to handle, about 2 minutes. Peel the eggs

(recipe continues)

and cut them in half lengthwise. Separate the whites from the yolks. Coarsely chop the egg whites, and add them to the bowl with the chopped shrimp. Press the yolks through a mesh strainer into a medium bowl. Add the mayonnaise, hot sauce, mustard, and remaining ½ teaspoon salt to the yolks and whisk until the mixture has the consistency of cake batter, about 1 minute.

5 Using a rubber spatula, fold the yolk mixture into the shrimp mixture until the shrimp and egg whites are evenly coated with the deviled-egg dressing. Season with salt and pepper, and toss again. (Covered, the shrimp and deviled-egg salad will keep in the refrigerator for 2 days.)

6 To serve, load 2 slices of tomato and 1 leaf of lettuce into each of the top-loading buns, and spread ¾ to 1 cup of the shrimp and deviled-egg salad into each roll. Garnish each roll liberally with the reserved diced bacon and the scallions.

MUSHROOM AND OKRA PURLOO

serves 4 as a main dish or 6 as a side dish
TIME: 15 minutes preparation, 35 minutes cooking

A purloo (or *perlo, pilau,* or *pilaf,* if you prefer) is a rice dish that enhances flavor by cooking the main ingredient—often a chicken or some other protein—and the rice together, all in the same pot. It's an efficient method that Karen Hess, in her definitive *The Carolina Rice Kitchen: The African Connection,* follows from its origins in Middle Eastern technique to northern Africa, to eastern Africa, and then to the colonial American South. If the liquid is calibrated correctly, the rice absorbs the flavors of the meat and ends up perfectly cooked, a one-pot meal.

We wanted to create a vegetable purloo that would bake deliciousness into the rice without a bird (the typical southern protein) so it could serve as a vegetarian main dish or as a side dish when some form of meat is already on the menu. And we wanted it to be every bit as luscious as the squab purloo from our first cookbook. This version features the meaty flavor of cremini mushrooms and poblano chiles, together with bright, fresh okra, but it works well with any number of veggie combinations, so long as the basic volume of vegetables remains the same. This dish is a perfect home for those three Brussels sprouts in the vegetable drawer, or that half an eggplant, or the last ear of corn (a dose of natural sweetness in the purloo is nice). Put the carrot half in there too, along with the celery tops.

8 ounces cremini mushrooms, trimmed and quartered (about 3 cups)

8 ounces okra, stems trimmed, pods sliced in half lengthwise (about 2 cups)

3 poblano peppers or 1 large green bell pepper, stemmed, seeded, and diced (about 2 cups)

2 teaspoons kosher salt

3 tablespoons peanut or other vegetable oil

2 medium yellow onions, diced (about 2 cups)

1 cup basmati rice, rinsed and drained

3 tablespoons chopped garlic (about 6 cloves), optional

2 large tomatoes, diced (about 3 cups), with any liquid

¼ teaspoon crushed dried red chile flakes

¼ teaspoon dried thyme leaves

¼ teaspoon freshly ground black pepper

2 bay leaves

¼ cup dry white wine

2 cups vegetable broth, homemade (page 104) or store-bought

1. Heat the oven to 375°F, with a rack positioned in the top third of the oven.

2. Toss the mushrooms, okra, poblanos, and 1 teaspoon of the salt together in a mixing bowl, and reserve.

3. Pour the oil into a heavy-bottomed 3-quart Dutch oven or ovenproof pot set over medium-high heat. When the oil starts to shimmer, add the onions and remaining 1 teaspoon salt, and sauté, stirring occasionally, until they just begin to acquire some golden color, about 6 minutes. Add the rice and garlic, and stir constantly for about 2 minutes, until the rice smells toasty and the garlic begins to brown. Add the chopped tomatoes, with any liquid that collected beneath them, and the chile flakes, thyme, black pepper, and bay leaves. Stir constantly for about 2 minutes, until the tomatoes are well incorporated and beginning to dissolve. Add the white wine and the broth, and use a wooden spoon to stir up any caramelized garlic sticking to the bottom of the pot. At this point the contents of the pot will resemble a watery tomato stew.

4. In thirds, gently fold the mushrooms, okra, and poblanos into the pot. It may seem like too much vegetable matter, but fret not—it will cook down and reduce, releasing liquid in the process. When the liquid returns to a simmer, cover the pot and place it in the oven. Bake for 20 minutes without opening the door.

5. Transfer the pot to a trivet, but leave it covered (don't peek!) and undisturbed for 10 minutes. Then ring the dinner bell.

AUSTIN-STYLE BRUNCH: GREENS AND EGGS *MIGAS*

serves 4 · TIME: 25 minutes preparation, 10 minutes cooking

Every southern city worth its salt has at least one culinary icon. Charleston's got a few: shrimp and grits, she-crab soup, benne wafers. Austin, Texas, has barbecued sausage and *migas,* a Tex-Mex entrant in the comfort-food canon that's served without fanfare at countless diners, family restaurants, and greasy spoons, but that also gets interpreted by fancy-pants chefs all over the Lone Star State.

Migas means "crumbs" in Spanish, and the roots of the dish can be traced to the Old World, specifically to Portugal and Spain. Popular legend has it that the *migas* we know and love—a fry-up of eggs, onions, fresh chiles, and tortilla chips, typically sluiced with a tomato salsa—was introduced to the United States by Mexican immigrants to Texas, who needed to make use of stale corn tortillas they couldn't bear to discard.

However the dish came about, *migas* is a dynamite hangover remedy and brunch dish. In our kitchen, we lay *migas* over Collard Greens with Poblano Chiles and Chorizo (page 146), and it's a powerful restorative at breakfast time or at any time of day. As it happens, we've come to make this dish most frequently at suppertime.

¼ cup canola oil

Three 6-inch corn tortillas, cut pizza-style into 8 triangles

¾ teaspoon kosher salt, plus more to taste

2 tablespoons unsalted butter

1 medium onion, chopped

8 large eggs, beaten

4 ounces extra-sharp cheddar cheese, finely grated (about 1 cup)

1 recipe Collard Greens with Poblano Chiles and Chorizo (page 146), warm

Fresh or store-bought salsa, for serving

Heat the oil and one of the small tortilla triangles in a large skillet or sauté pan over medium-high heat until the tortilla sizzles vigorously. Add the remaining tortilla pieces and stir them in the hot oil until they become crispy and gently browned, about 3 minutes. Using a slotted metal spoon, transfer them to a plate lined with a double thickness of paper towels. Sprinkle with ¼ teaspoon of the salt, and set aside.

2   Pour off the oil, and add the butter to the skillet, and when it's completely melted and frothing, add the onion and the remaining ½ teaspoon salt. Cook until the onion is soft, about 8 minutes. Add the eggs and the tortilla chips, and scramble until the eggs are curdy but still moist, about 2 minutes. Sprinkle the cheese over the top, cover, and cook just until the cheese melts, about 45 seconds.

3   Divide the collard greens with poblanos and chorizo among the 4 warm serving plates, and top each portion with eggs and spoonfuls of salsa.

PAN-FRIED WHITING WITH PICKLED PEPPERS AND ONIONS

serves 4   TIME: **30 minutes**

hiles and fish is a natural pairing in the coastal tropics, and a fish like whiting, which is almost as sweet as shrimp, medium-rich, and fairly plentiful in North American markets, is the perfect choice for this recipe, though flounder or tilapia would also perform well. We like the earthy flavor of just a little orange habanero mixed with the much milder green jalapeño, but as always, tune the peppers to your tolerance and to the ingredients you have on hand. One of us inevitably takes a microscopic taste—yeow!—of the raw chiles we've purchased in an attempt to calibrate our seasoning. Heat levels vary wildly out there: we've encountered jalapeños that were as unspicy as an apple. And there's only one way to know for sure!

We lightly fry the fish with a minimal flour dredge in an oil seasoned with the flavor of the softened onions, peppers, and herbs, which will become a warm topping for the fillet on the plate. A generous shot of vinegar in the garnish keeps the dish bright and lively. Serve it with hot white rice, grits, or Toasted Rice and Peas "Hoppin' John" (page 157).

ONIONS AND PEPPERS

½ cup extra-virgin olive oil

5 cloves garlic, crushed, peeled, and cut in half

1 large white onion, sliced very thin

2 jalapeño peppers, seeded and thinly sliced lengthwise

1 small habanero pepper, seeded and quartered (optional)

1 tablespoon fresh thyme leaves, or 1 teaspoon dried

1 teaspoon dried oregano

2 teaspoons kosher salt, plus more to taste

3 tablespoons red wine vinegar white wine vinegar, or champagne vinegar

FISH

¼ cup sifted all-purpose flour

2 tablespoons white or yellow stone-ground cornmeal

1½ teaspoons iodized salt or fine sea salt

1 teaspoon freshly ground black pepper

4 whiting fillets (about 1 pound total), picked over for stray bones

---

Heat the olive oil in a 12-inch skillet over medium heat. When the oil starts to ripple, add the garlic, onion, jalapeños, habanero, thyme, and oregano and gently sauté, stirring occasionally, until the onions are translucent but not browned and the jalapeños have faded to olive green, about 8 minutes. Add the kosher salt and vinegar, stir for 1 minute more, and then remove from the heat. Allow the mixture to cool in the skillet briefly while you dredge the fish fillets.

(recipe continues)

1 Heat the oven to 425°F with a rack positioned in the middle of the oven.

2 Combine the onion, carrot, and potatoes in a medium cast-iron skillet or
   2-quart ovenproof baking dish. Drizzle the olive oil over the vegetables,
   sprinkle with ½ teaspoon of the salt and ¼ teaspoon of the black pepper,
   and toss until they're evenly coated with the oil and seasonings. Place the
   chicken, breast side down, on the vegetables and squeeze one lemon half
   all over the back. Season the chicken with ½ teaspoon of the salt and
   ¼ teaspoon of the black pepper. Roast for 20 minutes, then remove briefly
   from the oven.

3 Lift the bird (you may prefer to transfer it to a cutting board), pour the
   broth and wine over the vegetables in the pan, and move them around a
   bit with a wooden spoon. Using two sets of tongs, or one set of tongs and
   a large metal spoon inserted in the cavity, flip the bird over so that it is
   breast side up. Squeeze the remaining lemon half over the chicken and
   season it with the remaining 1 teaspoon salt and ¼ teaspoon black pepper.
   Roast until the skin is nicely browned on top, about 40 minutes.

4 Transfer the chicken to a cutting board, tent it loosely with aluminum foil,
   and let it rest for 10 minutes. Carve the chicken and serve with the pan
   vegetables and spoonfuls of the lemony pan sauce.

PORK LOIN CHOPS
WITH MUSHROOM CHUTNEY

serves 4 · TIME: 25 minutes

Pork chops were a mainstay of Lee family school-night cooking when we were growing up, and although our parents rarely seasoned them with anything more than salt and black pepper, we'd suck the bones clean. We're still ravenous for pork chops, and this quick mushroom chutney, sweetened with prunes and spiked with ginger, somehow encourages us to take the chop route more frequently.

Consider making this mushroom chutney for your favorite cut of pork; it enhances anything—even bacon!—with its earthy, wintry personality.

2 teaspoons kosher salt	1 tablespoon canola, peanut, or vegetable oil	6 ounces button mushrooms, quartered (about 3 cups)
1 teaspoon freshly ground black pepper	3 tablespoons unsalted butter	6 ounces shiitake or cremini mushrooms, woody stems trimmed, cut into eighths (about 2 cups)
1 teaspoon sifted all-purpose flour	1 tablespoon grated peeled fresh ginger	
4 bone-in pork loin chops (each 1¼ inches thick; about 2½ pounds total)	1 medium yellow onion, chopped (about ¾ cup)	2 tablespoons dark brown sugar
	6 ounces pitted prunes, quartered (about 1¼ cups)	½ cup red wine vinegar

1 Heat the oven to 425°F.

2 In a small bowl, mix 1 teaspoon of the salt, the black pepper, and the flour together. Sprinkle half of the mixture over one side of each pork chop.

3 Pour the oil into a 12-inch cast-iron skillet or ovenproof sauté pan and heat it over high heat until the first wisp of smoke rises. Tilt the skillet gently in a circular motion so the oil coats the bottom thinly and evenly. Put the chops, seasoned side down, in the hot skillet (take care not to crowd them in the pan; sear them in batches of two, if necessary) and sprinkle the remaining half of the seasoning mixture on the sides facing up. Sear the pork chops until they are a rich golden brown, turning them when the first side is done, about 3 minutes per side.

4 Turn the chops so the first side faces down again, and transfer the skillet to the oven. Bake for 2 minutes for rare, 4 minutes for medium-rare, and 6 minutes for well-done. Remove the skillet from the oven, transfer the chops to a large plate or platter, and tent them with aluminum foil.

5 Add the butter, ginger, onion, prunes, button and shiitake mushrooms, and the remaining 1 teaspoon salt to the skillet, and place it over medium heat. Stir with a wooden spoon, scraping any caramelized pork bits off the bottom, and sauté, stirring, until the onion softens slightly and the surface of the mushrooms has begun to sweat a bit, about 3 minutes. Add the brown sugar, vinegar, and ½ cup water, and continue to cook over low heat until the vegetables have achieved an even degree of softness and the liquid in the pan is syrupy, about 6 minutes.

6 Divide the pork chops among 4 warm dinner plates, and spoon the mushroom chutney liberally over and around the chops.

SMOKED TROUT

serves 4 · TIME: 15 minutes

The delicate, earthy flavor of America's finest freshwater swimmer takes to smoke exceptionally well. Fragrant smoked trout makes some fantastic light midweek meals: serve it as a sandwich spread (blend with just enough cream cheese to bind), or offer it up as a whole warm fillet, fresh from the smoker, alongside a heap of greens and a cup of soup. Trout is elegant enough for company and readily available year-round, since it is often farm-raised (the vast majority of American trout are raised in Idaho and North Carolina, and the vast majority of these are rainbow trout). It's a sustainable seafood choice.

If you don't have a household smoker (which resembles an aluminum roasting pan with a tight-fitting lid), a roasting pan covered with foil works well. This recipe calls for a brisk, hot smoking for 10 minutes on top of the stove, which is effective and speedy but requires a little more vigilance (hot pan!) than smoking in the oven. Once you locate a source for the finely ground wood chips that stovetop smoking requires, and become comfortable with the basic technique, you'll find yourself performing this trick on any number of proteins and vegetables—like Smoked Cauliflower (page 166), one of our favorites. And although we eat this smoked trout most often as a main course, it makes a superb cocktail-hour snack for 6 to 8 people, served with crackers and garnished with capers and wedges of lemon, or an appetizer salad for 4, flaked over small plates of dressed fresh greens.

If you've never used a stovetop smoker, or even if you have, read Notes on Successful Stovetop Smoking, page 98.

---

4 whole trout fillets	½ teaspoon freshly ground black pepper	I large lemon, cut into wedges
½ teaspoon kosher salt		

Put 2 tablespoons applewood or cherrywood smoking chips in the center of a stovetop smoker pan, or in the center of a 9-x-13-inch stainless steel or aluminum roasting pan. If you are using a smoker pan, place the drip tray and rack inside the pan. If you are using a conventional roasting pan and rack, wrap the roasting rack in aluminum foil and place it in the pan. Season both sides of the trout with the salt and black pepper, and place the fillets, skin side down, on the rack. Partially cover the smoker; if using a roasting pan, cover it with aluminum foil, crimping the edges tightly but leaving one corner uncrimped.

2 Turn a burner to medium heat, and center the pan on it. When you see the first wisp of smoke rise from the smoker or pan, cover it completely and continue to smoke the trout until the fish is opaque at its thickest part, about 10 minutes.

3 Serve with lemon wedges. (Covered, the smoked trout will keep in the refrigerator for about 2 days; warm it in a 200°F oven before serving.)

GRAN'S FLANK STEAK

serves 4 · TIME: I hour marination, 6 minutes cooking, 10 minutes resting

Although our ninety-seven-year-old grandmother, Elizabeth Maxwell, stopped cooking more than a decade ago, she continues to be an inspiration in the kitchen. For more than 20 years, she hosted legendary parties in the small Charleston kitchen house she rented at 43½ Meeting Street. Gran loved her recipes—fresh button mushrooms marinated for a day in red wine vinegar, dried tarragon, and garlic; a cool, salsalike fresh tomato salad called "tomatoes émincé" that we devoured years before "salsa" became a household word. While not all of her recipes were successful—"Belmont Bisque," a concoction made of a can of beer, a can of tomato soup, and a can of pea soup, was as disgusting as it sounds!—this flank steak is our hands-down favorite. Simply marinated in soy and bourbon, the beef takes on an enormous, incomparable flavor. It also never fails to conjure up memories of Gran's parties, where silver-coiffed doyennes in furs mingled with College of Charleston music students in Metallica T-shirts.

This recipe is easy to memorize, easy to make, and easy to eat. There are rarely any leftovers, but in the event there are, the next day's steak sandwiches are killer on toast with sliced tomatoes and mayo.

½ cup soy sauce	½ teaspoon kosher salt	I tablespoon sherry vinegar, white wine vinegar, or red wine vinegar
½ cup Kentucky bourbon or Tennessee whiskey	¼ teaspoon freshly ground black pepper	
1¾ pounds beef flank steak	2 tablespoons cane syrup or honey	

1 Pour the soy sauce, bourbon, and ½ cup water into a broiler pan. Lay the steak in the pan and flip it a few times to agitate and mix the marinade and to coat the steak in the liquid. Let stand, covered, for 1 hour, turning it once at the half-hour mark.

2 Remove the steak from the marinade, pat it dry with two changes of paper towels, and then season it with the salt and black pepper. Reserve ½ cup of the marinade.

3 Turn the broiler on and position the broiler pan 4 inches beneath the heat source. Wait until a drop of water dropped into the pan sizzles, and then add the steak. Cook for 3 minutes on the first side. Then flip it and cook for 2 minutes on the second side for rare, 3 minutes for medium-rare. Transfer the steak to a cutting board, tent it with foil, and let it rest for 10 minutes.

4 While the steak rests, pour the reserved marinade into the broiler pan and bring to a boil over medium-high heat. Simmer until reduced by half, about 6 minutes. Add the cane syrup and vinegar, and cook for 1 minute until warmed through.

5 Slice the flank steak as thin as you can across the grain, and serve with the sauce.

EASY SHRIMP CREOLE

serves 4 · TIME: 12 minutes preparation, 30 minutes cooking

The Creole cuisine of Louisiana gets its vigor and flavor from the rich stew of cooking traditions—African, French, and Spanish—from which it emerged. The canon of Creole dishes is astoundingly delicious and has a deserved reputation for being a challenge to master: think gumbos, jambalayas, etouffées. Our take on the classic shrimp creole—a spicy tomato-based shrimp stew—uses about half as many ingredients as most recipes we've seen, yet scrimps not a bit on flavor: We begin building flavor with a quick shrimp stock, and we finish the stew with a pinch of smoked paprika and a dash of vinegar that draw an intense, almost ovenroasted flavor from the tomatoes. We serve this shrimp creole over hot white rice or grits—a simple family-style meal that would dazzle your boss, and her fancy friends, too.

1 pound headless large shell-on shrimp (26 to 30 per pound; see Notes on Deveining Shrimp, page 61, and Shrimp Shopping Notes, page 63)	6 ounces fresh hot pork sausage, casings removed	½ teaspoon freshly ground black pepper
1¼ teaspoons kosher salt	1 large white or yellow onion, chopped	½ teaspoon smoked paprika
1¾ pounds vine-ripened tomatoes (about 5 tomatoes)	3 cloves garlic, finely chopped	½ teaspoon crushed dried red chile flakes
	1 large poblano chile, seeded and diced (about 1 cup)	1 tablespoon red wine vinegar

1   Peel the shrimp and throw the shells into a small saucepan set over medium heat. Add 1 cup water and ¼ teaspoon of the salt, and simmer until reduced by half, 5 to 6 minutes.

2   While the shrimp stock simmers, core the tomatoes: Set a strainer over a medium bowl. Cut the tomatoes in half crosswise and, using your pinkie finger, tease the seeds out of the cavities of each half, letting them fall into the strainer. Tap the rim of the strainer against your palm for 30 seconds, until most of the flavorful gel clinging to the seeds dissolves and drips into the bowl. Discard the seeds. Chop the tomatoes; you should have 2 cups. Add them to the bowl with the tomato water.

3   Pitch the sausage into a heavy-bottomed 4-quart Dutch oven or pot set over medium-high heat, and cook, stirring and breaking up the sausage with a wooden spoon, until the pork is just browned and has rendered

some fat, about 6 minutes. Add the onion, garlic, poblano, remaining 1 teaspoon salt, the black pepper, paprika, and chile flakes. Cook, stirring and scraping up the browned bits on the bottom of the pan as the peppers and onions release their liquid, until the peppers and onions have softened, about 6 minutes.

4   Add the tomatoes and their juice and the strained shrimp broth, turn the heat to high, and cook until the tomatoes have completely collapsed into a red, bubbling stew, 6 to 8 minutes. Remove the pot from the heat and stir in the shrimp and vinegar. Cover and let stand for 3 minutes, until the shrimp are cooked through.

PORK TENDERLOINS WITH MADEIRA AND FIG GRAVY

serves 4 · TIME: 1 hour marination, 28 minutes cooking, 5 minutes resting

Sugar fig trees in Charleston ripen their soft, sublime fruit in late July, and you have to rush to harvest them before the birds and the squirrels swoop in. We've even met dogs that love the mellow, sweet flavor of ripe figs.

Thanks to the miracles of modern produce marketing, we can get fresh California figs almost year-round. They tend to be a bit more costly than the ones we plunder from neighborhood trees in downtown Charleston, but we're grateful to be able to prepare recipes like this one any time of the year. This dish looks best with purple-skinned varieties, but it's delicious with any kind of fresh fig you can find.

Pork tenderloin performs beautifully in simple recipes because it takes readily to marinades, sears willingly, and cooks quickly to a pinkish medium-rare in a hot oven.

---

1 cup dry Madeira or fino sherry

¼ cup red wine vinegar or sherry vinegar

6 cloves garlic, crushed and peeled

12 sprigs fresh thyme

2½ teaspoons kosher salt

2 pounds pork tenderloins

2 teaspoons peanut, canola, or vegetable oil

½ teaspoon freshly ground black pepper

3 tablespoons unsalted butter

2 large shallots, finely diced (about 1 cup)

1 teaspoon sifted all-purpose flour

1 pound fresh figs, trimmed and quartered (about 3 cups)

---

1   Pour the Madeira and the vinegar into a gallon-size locking food storage bag, and add the garlic, thyme, and 1 teaspoon of the salt. Seal the bag and agitate to combine. Add the pork tenderloins, reseal with as little air inside as possible, and turn the bag several times to coat the meat. Marinate at room temperature for 1 hour, turning the bag every 15 minutes. (Alternatively, you can use a baking dish, covered with plastic wrap, for marinating the pork.)

2   Heat the oven to 450°F with a rack positioned in the top third of the oven.

3   Transfer the tenderloins to a cutting board, reserving the marinade, and pat the meat dry with paper towels. Brush the tenderloins with 1 teaspoon of the oil, and season them with 1 teaspoon of the salt and the black

(recipe continues)

pepper. Heat the remaining 1 teaspoon oil in a large cast-iron skillet over high heat until it shimmers. Add the tenderloins and sear, turning them occasionally, until they are nicely browned, 5 to 6 minutes.

4   Transfer the tenderloins to a plate, and pour off any remaining oil in the pan. Add the butter and shallots to the pan, stirring until the butter has completely melted, and then add the remaining ½ teaspoon salt and the flour. Cook until the shallots have softened and are fragrant, about 3 minutes. Then add the figs and the reserved marinade (including the thyme and garlic), and bring to a simmer. Turn the heat to low, add the tenderloins to the skillet, and nestle them among the figs. Transfer the skillet to the oven and roast, turning the meat once, for about 12 minutes for medium-rare (an instant-read thermometer inserted into the middle of the stoutest part of the tenderloin should register 135°F) or 16 minutes for well-done.

5   Remove the skillet from the oven and let the tenderloins rest on a cutting board, loosely covered with foil, for 5 minutes. Then slice the tenderloins into ⅓- to ½-inch-thick medallions and arrange 4 to 6 medallions, overlapping, on each plate. Spoon a ladleful of the fig gravy over each serving.

DUCK BREASTS WITH RASPBERRIES AND ROSÉ

serves 2 · TIME: 25 minutes

Although we've never hunted ducks, we developed our taste for the birds because South Carolina is prime waterfowl hunt country, and most neighbors have a freezer stocked with ducks and doves that they dole out to good friends over the course of the off-season (which is most of the year, in fact; duck-hunting season includes the weekend after Thanksgiving and the two weeks from mid-December to just after New Year's Day).

Since we eat duck more often than we're given it, we buy wonderful farm-raised boneless duck breasts at meat markets. They tend to be larger than those of wild ducks, and fattier too. But they sear beautifully and cook up quickly, and they take to all kinds of sauces, especially ones made with fruit. The one we make here marries our favorite summertime berries with our favorite summertime wine.

2 large boneless duck breasts (10 to 14 ounces each)	12 ounces fresh raspberries (about 3 cups)	2 teaspoons red wine vinegar
¾ teaspoon kosher salt	⅓ cup finely diced shallot (about 1 large)	1 teaspoon extra-virgin olive oil
¼ teaspoon freshly ground black pepper	1 tablespoon fresh thyme leaves (from about 4 stems)	¼ cup rosé wine
		2 teaspoons sugar

1 Put the duck breasts on a small cutting board or a large plate, and pat them dry with paper towels. Score the skin and fat in parallel diagonal lines, making four or five ¼-inch-deep cuts on each breast. Season both sides with ½ teaspoon of the salt and the black pepper.

2 In a small bowl, toss 10 ounces (about 2½ cups) of the raspberries with the shallot, thyme, vinegar, oil, and remaining ¼ teaspoon salt. (Reserve the remaining raspberries for the garnish.)

3 Heat the oven to 450°F.

4 Place a large cast-iron skillet or ovenproof sauté pan over medium-high heat. When a drop of water sizzles in the skillet, add the duck breasts, skin side down, taking care not to crowd them, and sear until the surface is golden brown, 4 to 6 minutes. Turn the duck breasts over and spoon off

(recipe continues)

all but 2 tablespoons of the fat. Scatter the marinated berries among them, transfer the skillet to the oven, and roast for 6 minutes for rare, 8 minutes for medium-rare. Transfer the duck to a cutting board and loosely tent it with aluminum foil.

5   Add the wine and sugar to the skillet and cook over medium-high heat until the berries have collapsed and the wine has reduced to a thick syrup, about 2 minutes. Strain the sauce through a medium-fine strainer to remove the seeds. Slice the duck breasts on the bias and serve them bathed in the berry sauce. Garnish with the reserved fresh raspberries.

GRILLADES AND GRAVY

serves 4 • TIME: 20 minutes preparation, 45 minutes cooking

City folk from Charleston and Atlanta to Houston have adopted this stellar veal dish, which has its roots in Cajun country. Like eggs benedict, grillades suit the laid-back, rib-sticking comfort-food spirit of brunch particularly well; both dishes combine simple pleasures (the eggs, the gravy) with indulgences (the hollandaise, the veal). But don't let that suggestion dissuade you from preparing grillades for any meal. The astonishingly good gravy, deeply seasoned with the veal juices and onion, is piquant from some multiplatform pepper action (pepper vinegar and crushed dried red chile flakes) and nearly steals the show. The visual perkiness of red bell pepper and the sliced scallion garnish livens up the brown playing field. Pork or beef round may be substituted, but veal is the favored meat. Serve grillades on top of grits or rice, and pair with a juicy pinot noir. If there are leftovers, serve them reheated, with a fried egg on top.

1½ pounds veal round, thinly sliced and pounded (as for scallopini)	3 tablespoons canola oil, peanut oil, or bacon fat	3 tablespoons pepper vinegar, or 2 tablespoons Tabasco sauce
¼ cup sifted all-purpose flour (1 ounce)	2 tablespoons unsalted butter	2 cloves garlic, minced
2 tablespoons white or yellow stone-ground cornmeal	2 medium yellow onions, chopped (about 2 cups)	2 cups chicken broth
1½ teaspoons iodized salt or fine sea salt, plus more to taste	1 red bell pepper, seeded and chopped (about 1 cup)	4 medium tomatoes, chopped (about 2 cups)
1 teaspoon freshly ground black pepper	6 scallions (about 1 bunch): 3 finely chopped halfway into the green; 3 thinly sliced, just an inch into the green, for garnish	1 teaspoon crushed dried red chile flakes

1   If the veal slices are unpounded, or are thicker than a stack of three nickels, then pound on them with glancing blows from the back of a clean heavy skillet, mallet, or rolling pin until they thin out some. Cut the larger pieces into strips approximately the size of an unfolded matchbook, 1½ to 2 inches wide by 3 to 3½ inches long.

2   Toss the flour, cornmeal, salt, and black pepper together in a bowl, and spread the mixture out on a large dinner plate. Coat each veal slice with the mixture, shaking off the excess.

3 Pour the oil into a 12-inch skillet and set it over medium-high heat. When
   a drop of water sizzles in the oil, cover the bottom of the skillet with veal
   slices. Fry for 2 minutes, until the slices have begun to lightly brown; then
   flip them over and fry for another minute. Lift the veal from the pan with
   a slotted spatula, and reserve in a bowl (to catch the juices and drippings).
   Repeat until all the veal is browned (it will be fully cooked later).

4 Add the butter to the drippings in the skillet, and once the butter foams,
   add the onions, bell pepper, and finely chopped scallions. Sauté, stirring
   occasionally with a wooden spoon, until the vegetables have softened,
   about 4 minutes. The onions may brown slightly. Stir in the pepper
   vinegar, garlic, broth, tomatoes, chile flakes, and the veal, along with any
   veal juices that may have collected in the bowl.

5 Cover the skillet and bring to a simmer. Then turn the heat to low,
   partially uncover the skillet, and maintain a low simmer for 30 minutes,
   stirring very occasionally, until the gravy has thickened noticeably. If it
   appears too thin for your taste, remove the cover and continue simmering,
   stirring constantly, for about 5 minutes more. Season with salt, if
   necessary, and serve scattered with the sliced scallions.

desserts

A sweet finish to a meal has the potential to do much more than just satisfy a craving. We're prepared to state that any type of dessert, well crafted, is better than none at all, but a well-chosen dessert—one that truly complements what came before—just might seal your reputation as an accomplished chef and entertainer. It's the final say, a way to complete the story that began with the first thing your guests put in their mouths. And if a dessert satisfies that craving in the lightest way possible, so much the better.

Making desserts is the one culinary pursuit in which otherwise staid people allow themselves to have some fun (of course to us, every part of the meal presents that opportunity). There's plenty of room in the canon of basic ingredients for you to get creative without turning unnecessarily complex (e.g., "Basil Profiteroles Injected with Peanut Liqueur and Garnished with Pop Rocks" is the type of dish better left to restaurants).

Buttermilk Pudding Cakes (page 229), muffin-size cakes with a soft middle and the lovely cheesecake tang of real buttermilk, are proof of this: none of the ingredients is unusual, they have all been combined in various ways before, and yet this formulation produces a cake that seems altogether original. And it's a wonderful secret weapon to add to your cooking arsenal, since the cakes serve as a springboard to so many other desserts when you add fruit or ice cream—you could even garnish them with Pop Rocks, if you insist. Use your imagination, with these basic recipes as a starting point.

CORNMEAL DROP-BISCUIT PEACH COBBLER (PAGE 217)

RECIPES

Cornmeal Drop-Biscuit Peach Cobbler

Fig and Bourbon Compote

Strawberries with Sour Cream
and Port Syrup

Cantaloupe with Black Pepper and Mint

Banana Pudding Parfaits

Buttermilk Pudding Cakes
with Sugared Raspberries

Brandied Plums

Peaches with Bourbon

New Fruit Salad with
Vanilla Fresh Cheese

Rice Pudding Pops

Black Walnut Ice Cream

Bourbon Vanilla Ice Cream

Jasmine Tea Ice Cream

Mint Julep Panna Cotta

CORNMEAL DROP-BISCUIT PEACH COBBLER

serves 4 to 6 • TIME: 10 minutes preparation, 25 minutes cooking

A summer cobbler is magic: peaches softening in their own sweet juice as a layer of biscuit dough bakes up to a tender, crisp crust. Don't let the ingredients list below fool you; it may appear long, but this cobbler is the simplest of impressive desserts—it packs all the comfort and wow-factor of pie with none of the crust-hustle, nor the hour-long cooking time. And in fact, this recipe rewards the messy hand because the cobbler truly looks most sensuous when you top the fruit with the dough patchily, so that the syrup bubbles through the crust in spots. For those with a bumper crop of summer berries—or for those who simply might not have a fresh bag of cornmeal in the pantry—a variation follows.

PEACH FILLING

2 pounds ripe freestone peaches (6 or 7 peaches), unpeeled, pitted, and cut into crescents (about 6 cups)

¾ cup packed dark brown sugar

2 tablespoons fresh lemon juice

2 tablespoons water (if the fruit is very ripe or overripe, omit the water)

½ teaspoon ground cinnamon

½ teaspoon kosher salt

CORNMEAL DROP-BISCUIT DOUGH

¾ cup sifted all-purpose flour (3 ounces)

¼ cup yellow or white fine stone-ground cornmeal

3 tablespoons dark brown sugar

1½ teaspoons baking powder

¼ teaspoon iodized salt or fine sea salt

3 tablespoons cold unsalted butter, cut into pieces, plus more for greasing the pan

½ cup cold whole or lowfat buttermilk

---

1 Heat the oven to 425°F.

2 Grease a 2-quart ovenproof dish with unsalted butter, and add the peaches, brown sugar, lemon juice, water (if using), cinnamon, and salt. Toss until the peaches are evenly coated, and then let stand for 10 minutes while you prepare the drop-biscuit dough.

3 In a mixing bowl, sift together the flour, cornmeal, brown sugar, baking powder, and salt. Add the butter and cut it into the flour by pinching small amounts of the butter-flour mixture together between your fingertips, until the mixture resembles coarse meal with pea-size pieces of butter mixed throughout. Add the buttermilk, and stir with a rubber spatula for about 1 minute, until a tacky, wet dough comes together.

(recipe continues)

garnish it easy

• • •

*With store-bought
vanilla ice cream*

garnish it fancy

• • •

*With rum-flavored
whipped cream
(see page 225)*

4 Pat handfuls of the biscuit dough on top of the peach filling. The dough should be patchy and should not cover the entire surface. Bake until the syrup is bubbly and the biscuit top is alluringly browned, 20 to 25 minutes.

5 Serve warm scoops in small dessert bowls, ramekins, or cocktail glasses.

VARIATION

drop-biscuit summer berry cobbler Make another earthshaking cobbler with the following two substitutions:

- For the filling, substitute 6 cups (about 1½ pounds) summer berries such as blackberries, strawberries, raspberries, or a mixture thereof, for the peaches.

- For the biscuit topping, substitute sifted all-purpose flour for the cornmeal, so that the total quantity of flour in the biscuit topping is 1 cup.

FIG AND BOURBON COMPOTE

serves 4 • TIME: 5 minutes preparation, 10 minutes marination, 14 minutes cooking

This versatile compote makes a superb condiment for any cut of pork you care to serve, but when we spin it dessert-wise, we like to use it as a foundation. We place about ¾ cup of the warm figs and their syrup in a small bowl and then spoon a generous scoop of sweetened whipped cream or other topping over the fruit.

1 cup apple cider	1 tablespoon dark brown sugar	Sweetened whipped cream, crème fraîche, buttermilk ice cream, or Greek yogurt, for serving
⅔ cup Kentucky bourbon or Tennessee whiskey	10 ounces dried figs (about 2 cups), cut into quarters	

1   Pour the apple cider and bourbon into a small saucepan, and whisk the brown sugar into it (the sugar need not dissolve). Add the figs and let them soak and soften for 10 minutes.

2   Bring the fig and bourbon mixture to a simmer and cook, uncovered, until the figs have completely softened, about 10 minutes. Using a slotted spoon, transfer the figs to a medium bowl. Continue to simmer the sauce until it's reduced by half and becomes syrupy, about 4 minutes. Pour the syrup over the figs and serve warm, topped with whipped cream. (Covered, the compote will keep in the refrigerator for about 1 week.)

garnish it toasty
• • •
Crushed toasted peanuts or toasted benne (sesame) seeds—sprinkled over whichever dairy product you choose to place on top of the compote— will add a layer of both texture and flavor to this dessert.

STRAWBERRIES WITH
SOUR CREAM AND PORT SYRUP

serves 4 • TIME: 10 minutes

This dessert looks stunning and has loads of flavor, yet it's almost as easy to assemble as scooping store-bought ice cream. If the strawberries in your market are less than perfect, just soak them in the port syrup for 15 minutes, tossing every now and then, before serving; in no time, you can transform those firm, out-of-season supermarket strawberries into a real indulgence!

1½ cups tawny port ¼ cup sugar	1 pound fresh strawberries, rinsed, stemmed, and quartered (about 1 quart)	1 cup sour cream or crème fraîche

1 Pour the port into a sauté pan set over medium-high heat, add the sugar, and stir. Bring to a simmer, stirring, and continue to simmer until the sugar has completely dissolved and the liquid has reduced to about ½ cup, about 6 minutes. (Covered, port syrup will keep in the refrigerator for about 1 week; warm the syrup in a microwave before serving.)

2 Divide the strawberries among 4 bowls and top with dollops of sour cream. Pour about 2 tablespoons of the warm port syrup over each serving.

CANTALOUPE WITH BLACK PEPPER AND MINT

serves 8 • TIME: 10 minutes preparation, 30 minutes refrigeration

Cantaloupe Balls and Minted Cantaloupe are two super-quick dessert recipes found in many southern community cookbooks. The recipe for Cantaloupe Balls in *The Charlotte Cookbook*, published by the Charlotte, North Carolina, Junior League, calls for mint jelly, which must have been a more common ingredient in groceries and (perhaps homemade) on pantry shelves around the mid-century. We've found that authentic mint jelly can be difficult to find these days; the commercial brands are often made with artificial color and flavorings.

When we make our own easy cantaloupe dessert, we toss the melon balls in a small amount of mint simple syrup—which is very easy to make, using fresh mint, water, and sugar. Even if mint doesn't grow like a weed where you live, you can find fresh mint in most supermarkets year-round. If you're truly strapped for time, skip the syrup and simply snip a quantity of fresh mint to toss with the cantaloupe. We've added the black pepper for intrigue and because we love how it tempers the sweetness of the melon and the mint.

---

8 sprigs fresh mint	1 ripe 3-pound cantaloupe, halved and seeded (see Cantaloupe Shopping Notes, below)	Coarsely ground black pepper
6 tablespoons sugar		
⅛ teaspoon kosher salt		

---

cantaloupe shopping notes ⋯ Selecting a ripe cantaloupe is easy. You simply find the stem end of the melon and sniff it the way you would a glass of wine. A ripe melon will smell just like the flavor of cantaloupe; an unripe melon will have no aroma. You can double-check by pressing your thumb gently against the opposite end of the melon; the surface should give slightly, but not so much that the skin is pierced. If it is, the melon is way overripe.

(recipe continues)

1 Strip the leaves from 6 of the mint sprigs and put the leaves in a small saucepan. Add 3 tablespoons water, the sugar, and the salt, and set the pan over low heat. Stir with a wooden spoon, bruising the mint against the sugar with the back of the spoon until the sugar has dissolved completely and the mint leaves have shriveled and are no longer bright green, 5 to 6 minutes. Remove the pan from the heat, cover it, and set aside in a cool spot.

2 While the syrup cools, use a 1-inch melon baller to scoop out the cantaloupe, letting the balls fall into a large bowl; you should have about 1 quart melon balls.

3 When the mint syrup is cool enough to touch, strain it into the cantaloupe in the bowl, and toss to coat. Grind black pepper over the melon to taste, and chill in the refrigerator, covered, for 30 minutes or up to 2 days.

4 Strip the leaves from the remaining 2 mint stems. Toss the cantaloupe in the bowl, and serve the cantaloupe and syrup in tumblers or bowls, garnished with the fresh mint leaves.

BANANA PUDDING PARFAITS

serves 6 • TIME: 30 minutes preparation, 30 minutes cooling, 30 minutes refrigeration

Banana pudding is one of the South's most cherished twentieth-century desserts, and there are a million and one ways to make it. The recipe we grew up with, a staple of school lunchrooms, is made from a box of artificially flavored banana pudding in an aluminum pan with a few banana slices, Cool Whip on top, and a layer of Nilla Wafers. As any eight-year-old will tell you, it's good, but there are about ten missed opportunities there to boost and freshen up the flavor of this delicious dessert. Using real ingredients never hurt anyone!

For us, sweet concentrated banana needs a little lemon juice, to brighten and focus it and to keep it from seeming too cloying. Instead of trying to blend all the ingredients into a uniform pudding, we opt to prepare them separately—bananas, pudding, cream—and to layer them in a parfait glass, so the person eating the dessert gets to perform the finishing blend. Oh, and the contrasting crunch of cookies (so necessary to the success of any banana pudding) in our version is represented by veins of crushed gingersnaps, added between layers. The flavors of ginger, rum, and banana are a tropical troika to rival basil, mozzarella, and tomato.

And if you don't own parfait glasses, stemmed wineglasses will do perfectly. Anything but a foil pan!

BANANAS	CUSTARD	RUM-FLAVORED WHIPPED CREAM
2 pounds ripe bananas (about 5 large bananas), peeled and broken into pieces	3 cups whole milk	1 cup heavy cream
2 teaspoons fresh lemon juice	1 teaspoon pure vanilla extract	1 tablespoon sugar
2 teaspoons sugar	3 large eggs	2 tablespoons premium-quality dark rum, such as Mount Gay or Myers's
½ teaspoon kosher salt	¾ cup sugar	
	2 tablespoons cornstarch	¾ cup crushed gingersnaps (approximately 8 cookies)

1 Combine the bananas, lemon juice, sugar, and salt in a food processor and pulse until the mixture is a smooth puree. Press plastic wrap on the surface of the banana puree to prevent browning, and reserve in the fridge (it will keep for up to 24 hours).

(recipe continues)

2 Heat the milk and vanilla in a medium saucepan over medium-high heat until it just begins to steam. In a bowl, whisk the eggs with the sugar and cornstarch until evenly combined. Whisking constantly, pour the warm milk into the eggs in a thin stream; whisk until they're combined. Return the mixture to the saucepan and cook over medium heat, stirring until the custard is thick and bubbling, about 4 minutes. Transfer the custard to a bowl and let cool to room temperature. Refrigerate the custard, covered, until it is well chilled, about 30 minutes.

3 When you are ready to serve the dessert, whip the cream with the sugar and the rum until it forms stiff peaks. Layer the custard, banana puree, and cookie crumbles in parfait glasses until the glasses are two-thirds full. Finish with a generous dollop of whipped cream. Banana Pudding Parfaits will keep in the refrigerator for about 15 minutes before the gingersnap layer begins to become soggy. If you wish to keep the assembled parfaits in the fridge for up to 2 days, layer only the custard and banana puree in the glasses and cover them with plastic wrap; then, just before serving, finish each parfait with a layer of gingersnap crumbles and a dollop of whipped cream.

BUTTERMILK PUDDING CAKES WITH SUGARED RASPBERRIES

serves 8 • TIME: 15 minutes

These individual dessert cakes, which bake in less than 10 minutes in a standard nonstick muffin pan, combine the warming comfort of vanilla custard with the tangy righteousness of a buttermilk pound cake. We serve them hot, with sugar-dusted raspberries—the cakes' warmth softens the raspberries slightly, making them alluringly jammy. So simple, so delicious.

You'll note from the variations that follow that these cakes are true dessert heroes in our simple, fresh, southern kitchen. Often we'll go to the market knowing that this cake (which uses ingredients we wager are in your pantry already) will be the foundation for a riff on whatever fruit looks best that day.

If you don't own a nonstick muffin pan, spray your pan with cooking spray (or grease the pan with butter, then dust it with flour) before pouring in the batter.

BUTTERMILK PUDDING CAKES

¾ cup sifted all-purpose flour (3 ounces)

1½ teaspoons baking powder

2 large eggs

¾ cup whole or lowfat buttermilk

1 teaspoon pure vanilla extract

⅓ cup sugar

4 tablespoons (½ stick) unsalted butter, melted and cooled to room temperature

RASPBERRIES

8 ounces (2 cups) fresh raspberries

¼ cup sugar

Whipped cream (optional)

1 Heat the oven to 425°F with a rack positioned in the top third of the oven.

2 Sift the flour with the baking powder in a large bowl. In a second large bowl, beat the eggs with a whisk until creamy and yellow, and then whisk in the buttermilk, vanilla, sugar, and butter (the mixture will look curdy and broken; that is fine). Add the flour mixture to the egg mixture, and whisk until the batter is combined and smooth.

3 Divide the batter among 8 standard-size (3-ounce) nonstick muffin-pan cups, filling them two-thirds full. Bake for 9 minutes. Check the cakes by inserting a knife tip between the rim of the cake and the muffin cup and pulling gently to expose the side of the cake. If the side of the cake

(recipe continues)

appears evenly browned, the cakes will hold together when inverted and are ready. If not, bake for another minute and check again.

4   While the cakes bake, place the raspberries in a medium bowl. Shower them with the sugar, and then use your hand to gently toss them in the sugar until they have a light dusting on them. (If the berries are overripe and bursting, or wet because you washed them, the sugar will dissolve on them. This is fine—they'll still taste great!)

5   When the cakes are done, invert them onto individual small plates and divide the berries among them, mounding them on top and around the cakes, and top with a dollop of whipped cream, if using.

buttermilk pudding cake dessert ideas

SIMPLER

buttermilk pudding cakes with raspberry sauce and whipped cream Combine 8 ounces (2 cups) fresh raspberries, 3 tablespoons water, and 1 teaspoon sugar in a food processor, and puree. Place each cake on a small plate, top with a dollop of sweetened whipped cream, and pour the raspberry sauce over the whipped cream and cake until the sauce pools around it.

buttermilk pudding cakes au rhum Make a rum syrup by dissolving ½ cup sugar in ¼ cup water in a small saucepan set over low heat. Add ⅓ cup dark rum, such as Mount Gay, and stir to combine. Brush this mixture over the warm baked cakes 2 to 3 times, until soaked. Top with orange or grapefruit segments.

SIMPLE

buttermilk pudding cakes with brandied plums
Warm Brandied Plums (page 232) in a saucepan and cut them into slices. Serve each warm cake topped with 3 or 4 slices and a few spoonfuls of the plum-brandy syrup. Top with whipped cream, crème fraîche, sour cream, or a small scoop of store-bought vanilla ice cream.

buttermilk pudding cakes with strawberries in port wine syrup Make the port wine syrup as described in Strawberries with Sour Cream and Port Syrup (page 220, Step 1). Instead of drizzling the syrup over the strawberries, let the strawberries soak in it, tossing them every 5 minutes, for 15 minutes. Spoon this mixture over the cakes and then top with whipped cream, crème fraîche, or sour cream.

buttermilk pudding cakes with peaches with bourbon
Make the Peaches with Bourbon (page 234). Spoon peaches and syrup over each cake, and top with dollops of whipped cream sweetened to taste with sugar and bourbon.

BRANDIED PLUMS

makes two 1-quart jars ● TIME: 40 minutes, 30 minutes cooling

Fresh plums "pickled" with brandy, hot syrup, and spice are a southern tradition, and one of our favorite springboards to several quick desserts: a warm plum half nestled into a dish of vanilla ice cream, for example, or thinly sliced plums stuffed into crepes with a smear of Buttermilk Fresh Cheese (page 93).

And the syrup! The rose-colored elixir that remains in the jar is potent, fruity, mellow, and worth fighting over. A tablespoon at bedtime chases off bad dreams and any form of malaise. In a savory setting, the syrup can be used to baste and lacquer a roasting duck's gorgeous crackling skin. And brandied plum syrup inevitably finds its way into our Lowcountry Pousse-Rapière (page 40), a fizzy aperitif of plum syrup and sparkling wine.

3 pounds plums (about 12 large plums)	Two 1-inch-long pieces of cinnamon stick 2 cups sugar	¼ teaspoon kosher salt 2 cups VSOP (or better) brandy

1   Fill two 1-quart glass jars (ideally the French type, with the hinged clamp-down lid, which are particularly gift-worthy) with water. Place the jars in a deep stockpot, and fill the pot with water up to the shoulder of the jars, about an inch beneath their rims. Remove the jars from the pot and discard the water inside them. Bring the water in the pot to a boil.

2   While the water is heating, prepare the plums: Prick several holes around the stem ends of the plums. Pack the plums into the jars, quartering and pitting any plums that don't fit and placing the quartered pieces in the gaps between the whole plums. Add a cinnamon stick to each jar.

3   In a 2-quart saucepan or skillet, bring the sugar, salt, and 1 cup water to a boil. Then turn the heat to low and simmer for 10 minutes, stirring occasionally. Allow the syrup to cool for 10 minutes, then stir in the brandy. Immediately pour the liquid into the jars up to ½ inch from the rim.

4   Partially close each jar (to leave a gap for steam to escape), and place them in the pot of boiling water. Let the water boil for 10 minutes.

5   Carefully remove the jars with a jar lifter or two sets of tongs, and close the lids tightly. Cool to room temperature, about 30 minutes; then refrigerate for up to 2 weeks.

RICE PUDDING POPS

serves 6 • TIME: 35 minutes cooking, 30 minutes cooling, 4 hours freezing

Carolina Gold is the name given to an esteemed variety of rice that was brought to Charleston from Madagascar in the late 1600s. The rice was the Lowcountry's primary cash crop until the early twentieth century, and although these days rice is grown mostly by landowners who want to attract waterfowl, the region's taste for rice remains. *Charleston Receipts*, our hometown's seminal cookbook, contains some truly esoteric rice recipes: for rice breads and muffins, rice croquettes, and even a rice omelet.

These rice pudding popsicles are a cool new take on the warm, soothing classic. They've got an intense flavor—thanks to the aromatic jasmine or basmati rice we typically use—and an alluring texture. We often add yellow curry powder (a spice brought to the Lowcountry from Asia in the eighteenth century) or the Indian spice mixture garam masala to add intrigue. Feel free to use a more conventional rice pudding spice such as cinnamon, nutmeg, or ginger.

2 tablespoons unsalted butter	I quart whole milk	½ teaspoon garam masala, curry powder, ground cinnamon, or ground ginger, plus more to taste
½ cup long-grain jasmine or basmati rice	½ cup sugar, plus more to taste	
¼ teaspoon kosher salt, plus more to taste	I teaspoon pure vanilla extract	I large egg

1   In a heavy-bottomed 3-quart pot, melt the butter over medium heat, and when it is frothy, add the rice and salt. Cook, stirring and taking care to prevent the butter from browning, until the rice is very fragrant and opaque, about 2 minutes. Add the milk, sugar, vanilla, and garam masala, cover, turn heat to medium-high, and bring to a simmer. When the mixture starts to simmer, turn the heat to low and cook, covered, until the rice is completely tender, about 30 minutes.

2   Beat the egg in a large bowl. Pour the rice mixture in a thin stream into the bowl, whisking constantly to keep the egg from cooking. Season to taste with salt, sugar, and garam masala. Let the mixture cool to room temperature, about 30 minutes.

3   Pour the rice mixture into six 4-ounce popsicle molds, leaving ½ inch at the top of each mold for the custard to expand. Freeze as long as 4 hours.

(recipe continues)

4 To unmold the popsicles, hold the molds horizontally and run warm tap water briefly over the length of the popsicle molds, until the popsicles release.

VARIATIONS

hot rice pudding For soothing comfort on a chilly day, add an extra ¼ cup rice to the recipe. Just after adding the egg to the mixture, transfer the custard to small ramekins and serve.

cold rice pudding To cool down quickly on a hot day, simply chill the pudding at the end of Step 2 and serve it cold.

rice pudding ice cream After the rice custard has cooled to room temperature (at the end of Step 2), refrigerate it until it is very cold, about 4 hours. Then churn it in an ice cream maker according to the manufacturer's instructions.

BLACK WALNUT ICE CREAM

makes about 1½ pints; serves 6 • TIME: 15 minutes cooking, 4 hours refrigeration, 15 to 30 minutes churning, 2 hours freezing

The black walnut is a tree native to North America that produces copious softball-size green fruit that tend to drop in driveways and on lawns in the Midwest and throughout the southern Appalachians. The nuts inside are extremely difficult to crack, but those who persist—or who, like us, have a nut processor do the work for them—are richly rewarded.

Black walnuts have an exotic flavor that is unlike a common walnut, or any other nut really. They're almost too rich to eat out-of-hand—better to bake into cakes or churn into ice creams like this one. Since they're harvested by hand, black walnuts tend to be expensive (expect to pay up to $15 per pound). But a little goes a long way: a 1-pound bag would make about four batches of this ice cream. Most candy and nut stores carry them, but if there's not one in your area, try an Internet source such as boiledpeanuts.com or Hammons Products.

1 cup whole milk	2 cups cold heavy cream	¼ teaspoon kosher salt
½ cup sorghum syrup or maple syrup	¼ teaspoon pure almond extract	½ cup black walnuts, chopped
2 large egg yolks		

1 Pour the milk into a small saucepan set over medium heat, and whisk in the sorghum syrup. Beat the egg yolks in a large bowl. When the milk mixture reaches 150°F, pour it into the eggs in a thin stream, whisking constantly until the liquids are completely combined. Return the mixture to the pan and heat it over low heat, stirring, until the custard just coats the back of a spoon, or a candy thermometer reaches 175°F, 3 to 4 minutes.

2 Remove the pan from the heat and add the heavy cream, almond extract, and salt. Let cool to room temperature. Then transfer the custard to the refrigerator and chill until it is very cold, 4 hours or overnight.

(recipe continues)

3 Pour the custard into an ice cream maker and churn according to the manufacturer's instructions until the ice cream begins to become stiff and hold its shape (depending on how cold your custard is and the type of ice cream maker you are using, this will take 15 to 30 minutes). Add the walnuts slowly as it churns, and continue to churn until the nuts are distributed evenly throughout, about 5 minutes. Transfer the ice cream to a container with a tight-fitting lid and pat a sheet of plastic wrap directly over the surface. Cover the container and freeze the ice cream until it has hardened, at least 2 hours. (It will keep for up to 1 month.)

4 Remove the ice cream from the freezer 10 minutes before serving.

BOURBON VANILLA ICE CREAM

makes 1½ pints; serves 6 ▪ TIME: 20 minutes cooking, about 4 hours refrigeration, 15 to 30 minutes churning, 2 hours freezing

As much as we love bourbon—the barrel-aged whiskey made from corn (in combination with barley, rye, or wheat)—we love this ice cream even more. Something mysterious and wonderful happens when you concentrate the South's greatest spirit and marry it with cream. The process rounds out bourbon's rangy edges and ushers in a constellation of appealing nuances: caramel, smoked nuts, butterscotch, sweet corn, brown butter.

1 cup Kentucky bourbon or Tennessee whiskey	¼ teaspoon kosher salt	4 large egg yolks
⅓ cup sugar	1 teaspoon pure vanilla extract	1 cup cold whole milk
	2 cups heavy cream	

1 Pour the bourbon into a saucepan, bring it to a boil over medium-high heat, and add the sugar and salt. Stir until the sugar dissolves, about 2 minutes. Continue to boil over medium heat until the liquid is reduced by one fourth, about 6 minutes.

2 Add the vanilla and cream to the pan and heat over medium heat until a candy thermometer reads 150°F, 2 to 3 minutes. Beat the egg yolks in a large bowl, and pour the bourbon cream into the eggs in a thin stream, whisking constantly until the liquids are completely combined. Return the mixture to the pan and heat over low heat, stirring, until the custard just coats the back of a spoon, or a candy thermometer reaches 175°F, 3 to 4 minutes. Add the milk. Transfer the ice cream base to a pitcher or other container and refrigerate for 4 hours or overnight, until it is very cold.

3 Pour the chilled bourbon custard into an ice cream maker and churn according to the manufacturer's instructions. The ice cream should be the consistency of a very thick milkshake (depending on how cold your custard is and the type of ice cream maker you are using, this will take 15 to 30 minutes). Transfer the ice cream to a container with a tight-fitting lid, and pat a sheet of plastic wrap directly over the surface. Cover the container and freeze the ice cream until it has hardened, at least 2 hours. (It will keep for up to 1 month.)

4 Remove the ice cream from the freezer 10 minutes before serving.

JASMINE TEA ICE CREAM

makes about 1 quart; serves 8 • TIME: 30 minutes cooking, 4 hours refrigeration, 30 minutes churning, 2 hours freezing

Jasmine! This tropical shrub lends its exotic scent to many of the gardens and alleyways of downtown Charleston. One of the South's most famous flowers also happens to be one of the best herbal seasonings there is, with a bright, euphoric perfume and flavor—not as brooding or wintery as bergamot, the Mediterranean citrus that flavors Earl Grey tea. Fresh jasmine blossoms are added to tea blends (both green and oolong teas, but mostly green) throughout Asia to perfume the tea leaves.

In the United States, jasmine is underutilized outside of the province of tea, which is a shame, given how readily accessible a jasmine tea bag is at the grocery store. We've seasoned custards with jasmine tea quite successfully; a sorbet is the next challenge on our list. Serve this ice cream by itself as a palate cleanser or with slices of fresh mango. Or feel free to experiment, matching its floral qualities with tropical and fruity flavors, for example making a jasmine tea milkshake with a vein of softened passion-fruit gelato swirled into it.

| 3 large egg yolks | 6 regular-size jasmine tea bags | ¼ teaspoon kosher salt |
| 2¼ cups whole milk | ½ cup sugar | 1½ cups heavy cream |

1 Lightly beat the egg yolks in a medium bowl, and set it aside.

2 Pour the milk into a small saucepan and heat it over medium heat, stirring frequently, until small frothy bubbles begin to form on the surface, about 6 minutes and 140°F.

3 While the milk is heating, place the tea bags in a medium saucepan and add 2 tablespoons very hot tap water to soften the leaves.

4 When the milk has begun to froth, pour it over the tea and stir twice. Let steep for 2 minutes. Then remove the tea bags from the milk, pressing them lightly against the rim of the pan before discarding them.

5 Add the sugar and salt to the milk, and stir. Reheat the mixture over medium heat until it reaches 150°F. Then slowly pour the mixture in a thin stream, whisking constantly, into the bowl of beaten egg yolks.

6 Pour the mixture back into the saucepan. Add the heavy cream and heat over low heat, stirring constantly, until the custard just coats the back of a spoon, or a candy thermometer reaches 175°F, about 10 minutes. Transfer the custard to a pitcher or other container, and refrigerate for 4 hours or overnight, until the custard is very cold.

7 Pour the custard into an ice cream maker and churn according to the manufacturer's instructions, until the ice cream has the consistency of a very thick milkshake (depending on how cold your custard is and the type of ice cream maker you are using, this will take 15 to 30 minutes). Transfer the ice cream to a container with a tight-fitting lid and pat a sheet of plastic wrap directly over the surface. Cover the container and freeze the ice cream until it has hardened, at least 2 hours. (It will keep for up to 1 month.)

8 Remove the ice cream from the freezer 10 minutes before serving.

MINT JULEP PANNA COTTA

serves 6 • TIME: 45 minutes preparation, 1½ hours refrigeration

A spoonful of cool cream is the impression that a good panna cotta gives, without the roof-of-the-mouth-sticky impression of egg-based custards. We love the lightness and elegance of panna cotta ("cooked cream" in Italian), and like the Italians, we find that the dessert has an affinity for herbs—but only a touch, always in moderation. We've enjoyed sweet panna cotta gently seasoned with rosemary, but the one we developed with fresh mint is our household favorite. The vanilla-like character of bourbon adds its own inflection, but it's almost optional. (The flavor of mint to us has a Pavlovian association with bourbon, so much so that we're pretty sure we could get a buzz from mint tea!) This simple dessert is just the thing to finish a spicy meal of several courses.

1½ teaspoons unflavored gelatin powder (such as Knox gelatin)	2 cups heavy cream	¼ cup Kentucky bourbon or Tennessee whiskey
½ teaspoon canola oil	¼ cup sugar	
1 cup whole milk	1 cup packed fresh mint leaves, plus more for garnish	

1   In a small bowl, stir the gelatin into 3 tablespoons room-temperature water, and set it aside to soften. Pour the oil onto a paper towel and use it to lightly but completely coat 6 small (6-ounce) ramekins.

2   Combine the milk, cream, sugar, and mint leaves in a small saucepan and heat slowly over low heat, stirring occasionally. When the milk boils (about 30 minutes), remove the pan from the heat and skim the mint leaves from the milk with a slotted spoon. Discard the leaves.

3   In a 2-quart pot, bring the bourbon to a boil over medium heat, and boil for 30 seconds. Add the mint-flavored cream mixture and continue heating until the mixture reaches 175°F. Remove from the heat, add the gelatin, and stir well to dissolve the gelatin.

4   Decant the mixture into a pitcher or large measuring cup with a spout. Pour into the oiled ramekins and refrigerate until set, about 1½ hours.

5   Slip a thin knife around each ramekin to loosen the custard and then invert each custard onto its plate with a quick tap; serve immediately, garnished with mint. If serving later, keep the custards in their ramekins and press small swatches of plastic wrap directly over the surface of the custards and return them to the refrigerator for up to 2 days.

ACKNOWLEDGMENTS We are most grateful to Rica Allannic, Ashley Phillips, Jane Treuhaft, Stephanie Huntwork, Kate Tyler, Jill Browning, and everyone at Clarkson Potter who worked so diligently on *Simple Fresh Southern,* and to Pam Krauss, for bringing this cookbook to life.

And we offer our utmost and sincere thanks to the following, whose kind assistance was essential to the creation of these recipes and images: Quentin Bacon, Greta Barton, Allan Benton, Patrick Brantley, Jennifer Bryan, Mary Calhoun, Erin Clary, Donna and Robert Cox, Virginia Deerin, Wylie Dufresne, James Dunlinson, Nathalie Dupree, John T. Edge, Ben Fink, Cathy Forrester, Dorothea Benton Frank, Nichole Green, Janet Gregg, Bing and Kaki Guckenberger, James Haurey, Kate Hays, Janet Hopkins and Sarah Phillips, Josephine and Tom Hutcheson, Deepak and Annie Jain, Mary Johnson, Maggie and Hunter Kennedy, Jamie Kimm, Whitney Lawson, Erik Lopez, Wayne Magwood, David McCormick, Mindy Merrell and R. B. Quinn, Sarah Gray Miller and Tony Stamolis, Will Milner, Lawrence Mitchell, Alma Montague, Angie Mosier, Chris and Eve Pawelski, John Pelosi, Anne and Mason Pope, Lucinda Scala Quinn, David and Carol Rawle, Cheryl Rogowski, Bryan Simmons and Ralph Vetters, David Sullivan, Sam and Jan Van Norte, Valerie Van Norte, The Vegetable Bin, Capers White, Jonathan White, Ellen Wiley, Jaime Wolf, Barbara Zimmerman.

And to our loyal supporters, who have made substantial and generous contributions to our lives in recent years, and set this book in motion.

And to E. V. Day, Gia Papini Lee, Willy and Liza Lee, Caroline Lee, Elizabeth Maxwell, John Maxwell and Dora Keogh, and Mary and Kenneth Gellhaus.

INDEX

Note: Page references in *italics* refer to photographs.